CHUCKLEHEAD

Thomas Wells
Chucklehead

Published by Spines
ISBN: 979-8-89383-939-5

CHUCKLEHEAD

A FEEL-GOOD GHOST STORY WITH LAUGHTER
AND ROMANCE

THOMAS ERWIN WELLS

CHAPTER

ONE

After the heat of August has drawn its last scorched breath, and September comes.

When the world slows down to a crawl after harvest is in. That time of year when porch swings come back to life, and their well-worn chains creek like the bones of old folks. It's that time of year that this rolling tumbling story of fact and fiction begins.

It is the time of year when geese make long furling arrows in an Autumn sky. On faith and instinct alone, they ride the up drafts to a place above the world, where a built-in homing device designed by God's own hand, leads them a thousand miles beyond the horizon, to a place where fowl of the air may Winter out through the short days, and long nights of Winter.

That time of year when chattering squirrels can often

be heard barking with fervent joy as they store up their own brand of earthly treasure. Each for himself, and for his family.

Even though the squirrel does not sow, still at harvest, yet so does he reap. This... by intelligent design. No... not from the hand of man does he eat, but from the hand of Heaven's own architect.

Even though I do extract a great deal of joy from all four seasons, Fall is my favorite. I'm always ready for Autumn to shine her harvest moon.

Soon the grass will brown beneath my feet, and leaves will fall. Cold winds will usher in Jack Frost's icy breath, along with his unrelenting passion for nipping toes... and biting fingers.

Fields will become fallow, yet even the earthworm knows by instinct, that life will renew itself in the coming Spring.

Meanwhile... there are flannel shirts... chili and crackers... pinto beans and cornbread. And of course, sipping whiskey for a nightcap just before bedtime.

Whiskey softens the pain that loneliness brings when I'm all by myself, which is often, though I do have the occasional guest.

Actually, I do my 'best thinking' when I'm alone by the wood stove as it pops and glows. That seems to be when the Spirit of blended whiskey blends with my own Spirit, and each Spirit in turn, is glad for the other.

Just knowing that eggnog will soon be stocked in the dairy case at Jeter Market... And that I can buy the wonderful creamy elixir right up until New Year, gives me a childlike anticipation when the holiday season rolls around. Joy in a quart sized bottle... what's not to love?

Still in all, my biggest delight of Autumn surrounds a large black cast iron stove that I rescued just before Kansas City Southern tore down the old railroad depot, adjacent to my property. That was back in my first Winter here in Jeter.

The antique stove has seen its fair share of Kansas Winters. The foundry mark reads 1861. That means the ancient stove warmed the old railway station through the Civil War.

I reinstall the stove each year after first frost, and before the first hard freeze every Winter, or at least I've managed too so far. Though it is a strenuous task, and oft times requires a visit to the chiropractor, it is a task I do take a great deal of pride in.

On a date predicted by the 'Farmer's Almanac', I rise early on that morning, and watch the new day come. As it does, I scribble on a scrap of paper a detailed list of everything I'll need to reinstall the stove. Fortunately, everything I need is available from the friendly folks at Chalmer's Hardware.

After the sun has overcome the darkness, I let Jazzy out so she can do her duty.

She likely will participate in an early morning ritual between herself, and the resident rabbit. A game of cat and mouse. A rivalry they both seem to enjoy!

Good Lord willing and the creek don't rise, me and Jazz will be setting in the parking lot at Chalmer's Hardware when the 'OPEN' sign begins to flash.

First, I choose four lengths of gun barrel blue stove pipe and put them in the buggy. Then I roll to the 'fastener isle'. I meander through the metal bins until I find exactly what I'm looking for. Self-tapping stainless-steel screws. (Commercial grade of course.)

I count them out one by one. I buy enough to secure each length of pipe with three screws per joint, plus three more to hold the rain cap securely against the bone chilling winds of a typical Kansas winter.

I consider myself to be an honest man by most any man's measure, but larceny lurks in the heart of every man. I slip a couple of screws in my breast pocket just in case I have miscalculated or end up one way or the other being just one screw short. I don't mind being two screws short, but oh… how I hate being only one screw short!

Maybe somewhere in the darkest part of me, lurks a mastermind criminal! Sometimes I think I steal a couple of screws just for the pure dee ole debauchery of it! After all, who do you know that don't like to get one over on "The Man," once in a while?

I depart from the "Fastener Isle" on fast rolling wheels headed toward a corner in the very back of the store by the restrooms. This I do in effort to outrun the hot flush I feel creeping up my neck toward my ears.

I find a five-pound bag of weed & feed and examine it with such intensity that my glasses slide down on my nose as I pretend to read the application instructions.

With my ears still blushing like vine ripened tomatoes, I intermittently scan the isles for persons walking toward me with that particular stride of authority that says...you're busted!

Somehow, I've always imagined that even before you see the blinding flash of his shield shaped badge… even before you hear the "Loss Prevention Agent" address you in his well-rehearsed tone...

"Pardon me Sir, my security cameras indicate that you slipped something in your left breast pocket on isle 10. Would you mind emptying your pockets for me please?"

This thought totally unnerves me as fear spins my imagination out of control and leaves me completely unhinged. I can almost hear the unmistakable click of hand cuffs! Even though I see no indication that my annual theft of screws has been detected, I feel my Spirit depart from my body. From a safe distance, I stare back at myself in disgust! While trying to procure a believable alibi, I hear myself being chastised by my own conscious.

Once again… like years previous, I come to the realization that I don't have a criminal mind for shit! I attribute this conclusion to the very fact that my mind is not diabolical enough to even conjure up a believable lie!

Even though my glasses have slid down on my nose in the guise of false concentration, it is obvious even to my own self, that I look guilty as sin!

When my heart rate finally subsides, I stroll casually back to the (Stove Department.) On my arrival, I search the worn wooden bins for a new wire handled cast iron damper. My stove requires six-inch pipe to draw properly, and a six-inch damper to control the draw. Lastly, I choose the most conventional looking rain cap the hardware store has to offer, which is also usually the cheapest.

After checking my list for anything I may have forgotten, I find my only oversight. A roll of #9 wire to secure my stove pipe from the rain cap down to three equally spaced eyebolts on the roof.

The helpful hardware man leads me to isle #13 (which I fear is a bad omen.) He fishes out a roll of #9 wire holding it up like a man who has just found a needle in the haystack. He smirks with a prideful look on his face and asks. "Is this what you're looking for?" His tone is one of superiority. "That's exactly what I'm looking for!" Secretly in the throes of conspiracy I think to myself, "why you pompous ass! I should have stolen all your frickin' screws!"

After checking out, I guide the buggy through the automatic door and take a deep sweet breath of freedom! This I do only after scouring the parking lot for a

S.W.A.T. Team poised and ready to take me down and arrest me for fastener theft!

After the rush of debauchery has subsided, I drop the tail gate on Ole Blue, and strategically place the Winter's new stove pipe in such a way as to preserve its pristine condition.

The Ace Hardware bag containing all the fasteners, a new damper, and the #9 wire, goes in the passenger floorboard where it can be guarded by my little Black and White Papillon. She occupies the passenger's seat most everywhere I go.

As any good dog would do, she sniffs a couple of times, then reverts to her "loss prevention mode."

After we arrive home, and Ole Blue has been unloaded and the hardware has been stacked in the living room. When each piece has been arranged in its proper order of assembly on the living room rug, I pick up my phone and put in a call to my chiropractor.

Yesterday, after transporting the stove on a piano dolly, which rolls quite nicely on strips of plywood, I attached the motor hoist to the stove and lift it handily onto the back porch.

After careful alignment, and removing the back door, I turn the release valve on the motor hoist, and set it down gently.

Once the stove has been negotiated through the back door and down the hall to the living room, I attach the lion's claw feet, and shuffle it up on the red brick hearth where it will stand until Spring comes back around.

After the heavy work was done, I thought for sure that this year, I'd beaten Ole Doc out of a 5th of Jack Daniels Black Label... Jack Black, is our usual currency in trade. That's how I pay Doc when I need my back popped. That's how Doc pays me, when I plow his wife's garden. Once in Spring, then again every Fall.

"No such luck this year... My back feels like it's 'bone on bone!" My appointment with Doctor Fred is at 10 a.m. tomorrow morning.

I pop a beer and set down to a bologna sandwich while I dream of the first pot of pinto beans that will soon be boiling on the wood stove. I eat my sandwich and finish my first beer only to find that when I try, I can't stand up! Five beers later, I manage to struggle to my feet.

My Black and White terrier follows me faithfully as I wobble to the bedroom dragging one foot behind me like the 'Hunch Back of Notre Dame.'

I awoke this morning with my bedside radio still playing. This is quite the norm for me. From an early age, I set out on the road to become a famous songwriter... but it never happened. I followed that path for many years. I walked in the steps of all my high riding heroes' dragging my ole guitar and a transistor radio along with me everywhere I went.

Back in those days, when two roads diverged in a yellow wood? I'd look down one

as far as I could...Then I'd hot box the first freight car that slowed down enough to throw my ole guitar in, and still have enough time to hop up behind her.

Dawn found me the next morning at daybreak, sipping hot coffee and looking out the kitchen window toward the east. The lay of the land here in Kansas is so flat that a body can see all the way to where the world stops.

I watch as last season's crop of Amber wheat dances on a ghost wind as it skips across the lonesome prairie. Being as it's harvest time, it's as if the wheat were saying goodbye to the chaff.

I see the sun's first tendrils of this new day. There's not a cloud in the sky, so the sun sparkles exceedingly. The Golden beams of expectation are like the eyes of a fashion model, bursting forth in such a way, that no one with eyes that see, may deny attention to either.

The flecks wriggle and bounce like laser beams until alas, they aspire to their expectations, and erupt to super nova status. In all its majesty, a sleepy powder blue sky awakens. I watch as the sun comes up in full view. Once again, it has completed its journey from the other side of the world.

A mild chill had come in the night, giving notice that the sweet melody of songbirds will soon be gone. With no one to mimic, even the mockingbird will find its way to where the warm winds blow.

Blackbirds will wait like they always do. They wait like a procrastinating Hobo, until the north wind pushes them southward.

In the end, only crows will caw from leafless branches. Some crows won't leave until the snow flies. Some crows… and some Hobo's too.

Jazzy spins in a frenzied circle at the back door wanting out. She squats by the porch and pees, then she catches the scent of ole Mr. Cotton Tail. Jazz always gives him a run for his money. The rabbit on this particular day, circles around back the hen house in their daily game of cat and mouse.

Jazzy usually goes behind the hen house in hot pursuit. This time Ole Jazz fails to negotiate the turn and goes around the front of the hen house in order to avoid her nose being checkerboarded by chicken wire.

Mr. Cotton tail… he shoots up the middle like a linebacker at the Super Bowl... he all but runs slap dab over my Jazzy girl! Boy Howdy, how the fur did fly!

Jazzy, with the pride of a victorious hunter, lugs her kill on the right side, then on her left. She drags the plump furry creature up the steps and lays it at my feet.

The chicken wire didn't get her nose, but Mr. Cotton Tail sure did! I roll with laughter as the best little dog I ever owned, stands shaking with excitement.

"Good job Girl!" I preen like a proud Papa while

praising her. "Looks like rabbit and dumplings will be our first meal on the woodstove this year!"

After a few strokes across the whet stone with my butcher knife, I make a few strategic cuts and pull the britches off old Mr. Cotton tail. He barely fits in a gallon freezer bag. Then me and Jazz load up, and head for Doctor Fred's business address after stopping by "County Line Liquor" for a bottle of Jack Black to pay Doctor Fred with.

CHAPTER

TWO

Ole Doc likes our little arrangement. Mrs. Phillips draws a hard line on drinking. She poo-poos anything that might be viewed as sinful... or has the slightest tinge of anything that might be fun. Anything that might tarnish their outstanding... standing... in this little tight woven community is strictly forbidden!

Fred likes his whiskey, he likes his music, but truth be told... he loves his women. His, and mine, and yours too!

The combination of those three infectious addictions has fetched him a considerable amount of misery in the course of his life.

This includes... but is not limited to, three failed marriages, and just as many D.U.I.'s. A public drunk charge, one count of statutory rape, which got throwed outta' court... after a little palm greasing.

None of his offenses were anything serious. Actually,

they didn't add up to much of nothing but a hard row to hoe.

In the interim, Fred has racked up a goodly number of "Party Fouls." All this through several decades punctuated with a little jail time... and an endless stream of children, and the child support that has been aptly named for exactly what it is: "The fucking you get, for the fucking you got!

In the parking lot, I slip his whiskey up my coat sleeve, then I push through the office door and take a seat in the waiting room. I set hunched over my coat sleeve and stretch a pain-stricken grimace across my face. I'm not a hypochondriac, but I can fake me some pain just as good as the next one!

When I saw the curvy little Brunette behind the intake window, that's when I began to really put it on thick! I only got to set in the waiting room long enough to get in a good ogle at Doc's new receptionist.

Before I could get my eyes plum full, the nurse calls me back and says: "Lefty, did you hurt your arm this time?" "Yea, I say… but it ain't nothing Doc can't fix.

She leads me back to the examination room and announces my arrival. She gives me a pity-pat on the back, then closes the door on her way out. "Mornin' Doc" I say, while replacing my grimace with a smile. Doctor Philips tilts his Silver shorn head and asks in the whispering tone of conspiracy, "Did you bring it?" "Did I bring what?" Says I, as if I had forgotten his whiskey.

We both laugh as I pull the bottle from my coat sleeve. He rubs his hands together fiendishly, and pulls out two shot glasses, one from each britches pocket. Doc has always treated me like an old friend, even though we aren't. Actually, we've only set in with each other a few times there on stage at the Legion Hall.

I've yet to see Doc without his wife, except here at the office. I don't know if he likes the way I play and sing, or, If he knows I keep a bottle behind the seat of Ole Blue? Either way, he always invites me up on stage… and never fails to slug down a good hard pull off my bottle when his wife is in the Ladies Room.

Doc and I are both lifelong musicians, and both of us have seen our fair share
of glory days. Doctor Fred plays saxophone and can fairly make that thing wail!

"Hell to pay!" That's what we both were back in our younger days. I've always heard that it… "takes one to know one." 'Guess that's why we get on so...

"When you gonna' start hiring some young bucks to help you with that damned ole stove," he asks while pouring us a round. "Well Doc" Says I… "Cast iron breaks too easy to hire the football team. They don't call them the 'Jeeter Bulldogs for nothin' you know!"

Doc waves me over by the back stretcher table where we clink glasses and make a silent toast. He wears a screwed up and twisted expression on his face. I do as well. Both of us follow up with a head shaking shutter.

We exchange a conspiratorial smile, then he pours a second round to chase the first one down, then hides the bottle under the back stretcher table. He puts the shot glasses in his lab coat for easy access, then pats the back stretcher table signaling me to set… so I do.

His healing hands find my shoulders. Then his fingers course my back like a bird dog searching out a covey of quail. "Here's the trouble," he grumbles. Doc sets his feet like he's up to bat, and my back is home plate. Pain hits me hard like a foul ball in the catcher's crotch!

I feel several bones in my back pop simultaneously. First, I quiver with relief. Then, I feel my dead leg come back online. Doc is small, but his hands are strong as a vise!

"Been doing any gigs lately?" He ask curiously, while retrieving the shot glasses from his lab coat pocket.

"Not many" I say, as he pours another round. "Been playing the Fish Camp over in Smokey Hill some. I still play the Oasis over in Neaderville about once a month. I don't book like I used to, but I play whenever they call. "What about yourself, Doc?"

"Nope," he says in a forlorn voice. "Connie's been down with that knee of hers. The kids moved back home… and brought more with'em. If they ain't no rest for the wicked, he continued, then I must be the devil himself!"

Doc tipped his shot glass and swallowed hard… like he needed the burn. Then all of a sudden, a look washed over his face... like he was studying something out. He folded his arms and held his chin in one hand.

"I just thought of something Lefty. I saw Mayor Talby, down at the 'Tote-A-Poke just the other day. He wants me to put together a band for his birthday party... He said he'd go twelve hundred for a full band... Open bar and free food. You want in Lefty?" "Sure! Sounds like fun to me... don't it to you Doc?"

"Yea... it does! I need a little time off for bad behavior!" Doc gives me a halfcocked look that is soon accompanied by a shit eating grin, then his eyes begin to sparkle mischievously. I can almost see the gears turning in his head as he pours our fourth and final round.

"I'll get Warren Stinson to throw in some lead licks to sweeten things up if he's not already booked. There's a new preacher over at Whitwell First Baptist what can bend tarnation out of some guitar strings, plays that Telecaster till fire and brimstone all but come out of his amplifier... or so I hear. Nice young man they say... fresh out of seminary. He's an Ole Rock-N-Roller... least ways that's what I been hearing down at the Jeter Cafe."

"The Community Center ain't actually a bar, so maybe his young wife will let him bend some strings for us. If we have a Preacher in the band, and we're not playing at a bar, maybe Connie won't raise hell with me for taking the "gig. I'll pack up the ole lady and carry her to Church over at Whitwell next Sunday morning. She's been wanting to hear him preach anyway. I'll talk to the

Preacher and see if he's interested in making an extra couple hundred bucks. I figure he'll say, yes… two things I know about preachers; they love fried chicken… and they never turn down money."

"So, Doc, when is the Mayor's birthday party?" "November 14th." was the good doctor's reply. "Eight p.m. 'til midnight."

Doctor Fred led me back over to the back stretchin' table. "You know the routine; I need you to lay down this time Lefty." Doc commanded with a slightly drunken slur.

I laid down on the table, then he began to manipulate the foot switches. Soon I began to hear a series of snaps, crackles and pops. By the time he was done, I felt like a bowl of Rice Crispies.

There is a certain comfort I have with Doctor Phillips. Us making friends and all. Especially for a feller like myself, with a back like mine!

Doctor Fred… he's a little sneaky in the way he goes about things. He holds the back of my neck in one hand and rolls my head with the other. Then he starts up a conversation to keep my mind off what I already know is fixin' to happen. Even though I know, he always gets over on me anyway.

How'd you do with the truck patch this year Lefty? Hell with the truck patch, tell me about that little Brunette working up front... You been tappin' dat Doc?" (We both laugh.)

"Naw... She's a married woman Lefty!" He looks at me and tries to keep a straight face, but can't. (We laugh again.) "Now Doc, that ain't never stopped you before."

"Yea I know, but she works for me Lefty!"

"That ain't never stopped you neither Doc you ole Horn Dog!"

Before I even know what happened... it's over... "Man he's good!" Doc rolls me over for my final stretch. When I do stand up, I stand up straight. I've never left his office without feeling on top of the world... and... a couple inches taller!

CHAPTER

THREE

On the way home, Jazzy and I stop by to check the mail. The only time we do this, is when we're running low on gas. "Poskey's Full-Service Gas for Less." Jack Poskey is also the Postmaster. He is the proud papa of seven kids, all of them stair steps when they stand in a row. Being Mr. Poskey and his wife came from Sweden, so the kids are all toe headed too.

The only time I go inside the post office is when I have a parcel to sign for. Full service is exactly what you get at Poskey's. You ain't never seen the like! All you do is roll up, and roll down the window...

"Fill'er up?" Says one of the bowl cut toe heads. Want me to check under the hood?" asks another. "Sir, your left front tire only reads 26 lbs. but the rest have 32. I can fix that in a jiffy he exclaims while reaching for the air hose.

Another kid... a girl kid that shows all the signs she won't be a kid much longer, stands on a pickle bucket, and stretches gracefully across the hood of my truck washing the windshield. She shines it till it sparkles. Another toe head about seven, rushes up with a toothy grin, and hands me my mail. "Here you go Lefty."

These kids are like a pit crew! I pay the kid with the money belt which I assess to be the oldest boy, but younger than the girl. The girl brings Jazz a doggie treat, then we're on our way...but only after receiving a generous smile and hometown wave from the Crew Chief and proprietor. Mr. Jack Poskey.

We roll down Main Street past Jeter Inn and the volunteer fire department where we take a right hand turn up toward Town Square. Jeter's Town Square has all the trappings and mystique of a typical small town. The Courthouse is the center point of all that surrounds it. The massive cornerstones and great round marble pillars make it plain to all that behold it, the pure and simple truth... "Justice Will Stand!"

Quaint little coffee shops and eateries line the town square sidewalks. There are store fronts sporting everything from antiques to greeting cards.

"Jeter Music," has everything from guitar strings and woodwind instruments to Grand pianos and handmade hammer dulcimers from the Ozarks.

Our little community has become a tourist destination for its aesthetic beauty and the quirky little nuances that seem to draw tourists like gnomes are drawn to fairy dust. Jeter exudes an Ora of warmth and friendliness.

Around the first of each month, I leave Jazz home to guard the place while I ride down to the Square to get my ears lowered. I park Ole Blue in front of the candy-striped Barber Pole. The sign reads... "Corner Stop Barber Shop." This name befuddles me because the barber shop is not on a corner.

Actually, not a single business occupies a corner here on Town Square. In all reality, Town Square is anything but square. Even the park benches that surround the Court House are laid out on an arc.

In all its oddity, Town Square is not square at all, but shaped rather like "Churchill Downs!" The streets are curved, the sidewalks are curved, even some of the architecture, the old Library for instance, was planned by design with a radius included.

There are no STOP signs, because there are no corners. Traffic flows in and out of Town Square from only three equally spaced arteries. Each artery is equipped with a YIELD sign as you enter. When you exit Town Square there are no traffic signs at all, because none are needed.

On the far side of Town Square, we pass Jeter Market and Eisenhower Middle School. We go by the "Tote-A-Poke," where I wish they sold cold beer, but they don't, because they can't. The only thing I don't like about Jeter

Kansas, is that the city limits are inside a dry county. Other than that, it's like living in a picture book!

On the outskirts of town, we take the bridge headed home, and also, toward County Line Liquor. The bridge arches up to a considerable height, only to span a little of everything, but nothing in particular. The Missouri River runs through Kansas. So does the Arkansas, and Smokey Hill River. Most of our crops are irrigated by the Smokey Hill here in Jeter. Oddly enough, none of the rivers, nor any of their tributaries run beneath the bridge.

I've always wondered how that bridge came to be, or the reason for its existence. Only silos and grain elevators make their home below the bridge. Railroad tracks gleam like ribbons of steel when you look down from above. They run in pairs from here to there and most everywhere with a complex system of flags and lights and switch track plates.

Locomotives shuffle grain cars and cattle cars, tank cars and boxcars to and from their intended destinations with a choreography of dance that has been designed for but one single purpose. To load and unload train cars in the fastest, most efficient way possible. From the crest of the bridge, it's like looking down on a cluster of toy trains.

Norman Rockwell must surely have been the town's founder. This I assess due to Jeter's poetic nature and beauty. I see every brush stroke of his hand here. I see it painted on the Rosie cheeks of children when they play out of doors. I see it on the people of this hard-working community. I see it in their smiles when the workday is done. I see it in an Auburn sky when Kansas clouds choose to make it so.

I see it in a thousand different shades of Blue, whether it be painted on the sky, or in the faded overalls that farmers seem to be so keen on. I see earth tones that only Norman Rockwell, or Father Time, or maybe God could blend across the Smoky Hill River, as it treks across the land spreading life, and wealth, and a myriad of colors upon this tight knit little farming community that I have been so blessed to call home.

At night, I look up at a sky that seems to sweep so close to the earth, that even people who fear heights have been seen on step ladders, attempting to change the bulb on a burned-out star. Never have I seen a place with such heart.

Jeter could have chosen to be prosaic with the usual economy of design, but instead, Jeter chose to be poetic. Many of Jeter's roads have long sweeping curves that bank like a stockcar track. They are commonplace in our illustrious little town. A modest straight slab of concrete, poured and striped, would have served the purpose of transportation just as well.

The extra taxpayer cost that must have surely been incurred in the process of constructing such an extravagant highway system had to have been a significant burden on the town's people.

Even though the bridge that spans nothing in particular, may be a contradiction in terms when the word, "Span..." is used in its usual context, it does however span one's own self-imposed limitations between who we perceive ourselves to be, and who we can be when we apply the magical elixir of perseverance and imagination.

I have never failed to be inspired as I behold the magnificent view when I look in any direction from this bridge that was born not of necessity, but rather, from the necessity of being born!

Jeter Park can be seen from atop the bridge... so can the kidney-shaped duck pond, and the new library. What I like most when crossing the bridge is looking down on the monstrous conveyor belts, as they spew Golden waterfalls of wheat up hill. They fill one train car, then the next heaping full and running over, with Kansas' most precious commodity.

Just this side of 'County Line Liquor, we leave the highway and take a right. There, we cross the train tracks where the gravel road begins.

Outside of town the roads are laid out by the section. All roads outside of town are straight as a rule, and flatter than yesterday's beer.

Me... I only own three measly acres, which isn't much in this part of the country. My property does however sport a goodly number of shade trees. There's a cluster of

Red Oaks that form a canopy so thick that grass won't hardly grow beneath them.

There's a picnic table where I like to sit and play my guitar. It's a good cool place to work on broken down lawnmowers, and tillers, chainsaws and such. It was here when I bought the place. Off to one side, is a big brick Bar-B-Que pit that's seasoned in right nicely. I'd bet a dollar to a doughnut; it's fed a fair mess of farm hands in years past.

One day down at Jeter Cafe I met a feller what liked to throw horseshoes. He asked me if I like to throw shoes. I said that I did... and I do. Then he asked me if I like to drink beer. I said that I did... and I do. Then he wanted to know if I thought I could beat him at a game. I told him that I did, and that I was willing to wager on it! He bet me a 12 pack that I couldn't, and he was right! Ole Sammy Katz beat me like a Red headed stepchild!

I think maybe I was just a bit addled after old Sammy mentioned his last name was Katz. Even though I didn't mention her name to him, I figured he must be kin to Kory Katz, the first woman I laid with when I first came to Jeter. At any rate, on the way home from Sammy's house, I stopped by Chalmer's Hardware and bought me some throwin' shoes of my own.

The very next day I went up under the shade trees and drove me a pair of steaks in the ground. I made sure they were 40 feet apart, then I brought in a load of sand, and fixed me up some horseshoe pits.

I like throwin' shoes and drinking cold beer up underneath the shade when the dog days of Summer beat down so, that it's too dang hot for a body to do much else.

There's a good stand of Post Oaks out behind the truck patch, but they're in purdy bad shape. Bore worms, that's what the County Agent says. Some are dead and standing, and I know that's a shame, but Post Oak sure makes good heater wood.

There's a few Bur Oaks scattered here and there, and a couple of persimmon trees that don't bare much. What fruit they do bare, the birds and the opossums and the gal-dern squirrels fight over!

Standing stately on the edge of my property, is a windmill that used to supply the Kansas City Southern Train Depot with water needed to fill the thirsty boilers of yesteryear's steam powered locomotives. All three filling tanks are still standing, but only one looks like it might hold water.

The old windmill's blades are unusually large to produce the extra torque needed to pump water up hill. The round wooden tanks must be 20 feet from the ground to the bottom, then another 20 feet to the tank's rim where the water supply comes in. The County Agent said my well was the deepest in all of Jefferson County as far as anyone knew.

My home is nothing fancy, but I'm ever so thankful for

it. A place to call home is something I'd never really missed, because it's something I've never really had since childhood. When my eyes began to dim, and age came on me, having a home to call my own came to the forefront of all my desires. I've traveled most all my life, ever since music found me. I bought the place reasonable, and with owner financing. I tried for a loan at the bank, but a rolling stone gathers no moss, so I had no credit to speak of.

Ole Lester Kramer down at the Legion Hall, sold me the place on credit. Mr. Kramer seemed to like me from the get-go. He liked the way I played and sang and told jokes. The first time he heard me sing Hank Williams, he stuffed a twenty-dollar-bill in my shirt pocket.

Back when I first got to Jeter, I was road weary. The people here opened their arms to me, so I decided to hang around a while. Before I knew it, I was running a combine and harvesting wheat for Mr. Kramer. By the end of harvest, I'd saved enough for a down payment on the three acres.

I'd never owned much of anything except for a good pair of boots and a Stetson hat, and Daddy's old guitar. I've gone through a multitude of boots, and a goodly number of hats as well, but I'm proud to say I've owned only one guitar in my whole life.

Daddy gave me his old Martin D28 for my 13th birthday. I'm also proud to say I learned to play it well and make my way with it. Besides owning Daddy's old

Martin, owning property is the next best thing that ever happened to me!

I've got the better part of an acre fenced off and cultivated. I get my retirement check on the third of every month. With that, and what I make from the truck patch, and with a little guitar money on the side, I don't hurt for much of nothing.

CHAPTER

FOUR

It took a while to get the old house up to par. It had stood empty for a good long while. This place was Mr. Kramer's boyhood home. Young Lester Kramer took a job at the grain elevator back in high school. By the time he graduated, he'd learned the business of farming firsthand, from actual farmers. His aspirations were to attend Park University up in Kansas City and earn a degree in Agra business.

All that changed when a kindly old gentleman who had taken a liking to young Lester passed away. He left the boy a section of land to call his own. He also left Lester all the equipment needed to farm that section of land... all 640 acres of it.

After the windfall, Les married Lisa, his high school sweetheart. Together the two went about tending the soil and raising wheat. Les was too busy to go to school.

Instead of pursuing a degree in agribusiness, he found himself in the business of raising a crop of children, alongside a crop of wheat.

After me and Mr. Kramer signed the promissory note. I moved out of the Jeter Inn, and set up camp on my very own property. First, I pitched a cabin tent under the Red Oaks

by the picnic table and the Bar-B-Que pit. The first couple of days were spent combing the place in a drunken stupor in celebration of my good fortune and making plans for the new property.

Over the years, people had taken to using the place to dump trash that the city wouldn't pick up curbside. Old washers and dryers, swamp coolers and refrigerators, along with a vast variety of miscellaneous junk. I found several old lawnmowers that I pieced together, until I had one that would mow. Once I had a mower that worked, I began the arduous task of cutting three acres of waist high grass.

First, I mowed a spot big enough to drag all the dead appliances and scrap iron to. Then I mowed a spot big enough to burn old tree limbs and discarded boxes of mildewed clothes along with several old mattresses. I'd set fire to a pile of car tires, then I'd throw a mattress on the tire fire.

I must have set fire to enough tires, to burn a hole in the ozone!

Least ways, that's what the Fire Chief said... just before he handed me a citation for unlawful burning.

Most of the ole boys who rode in on the fire truck looked vaguely familiar to me, but they all knew exactly who I was. When I first hit town, I was still a working musician. I'd play every little Honky-Tonk and Dive Bar I could book in the surrounding counties. People in this part of the country work hard, and play even harder!

We all got to shootin' the shit and talking about this bartender Chick what works over at 'Dance A Go Go', and how she's one of the perks if you join the Jeter Volunteer Fire Department. And how a kiss from her is a part of a new volunteer's initiation.

After commonalities among men become greater than their differences, it sometimes happens that a softer solution to a problem that seems to have lost its urgency in the course of camaraderie, finds its way to the light of consideration.

When cooler heads have allowed themselves, 'due diligence,' sometimes the spirit of forgiveness steps forward, and wins the day.

"Well Lefty," says the Fire Chief. "Being as you're fresh out of tires to burn, and also a new property owner here in the county, I'm going to let you off with a verbal warning this time."

He reaches over and takes back the citation I'm still holding, and hands me a business card with a heading that says: "Permission to Burn." Just below the heading is a phone number to call so said permission can be granted or denied at the Fire Chief's discretion, with regard mostly to weather conditions.

It makes perfect sense to call first. When you call first, the fire department knows that the burn has been duly noted and is intentional. Below the phone number, are bullet points with a list of items prohibited from the burn pile. The first item on the; (DO NOT BURN) list is: Tires...

Below the list of things, you are not allowed to burn, is a mandatory list of things that must be done before starting the fire. Things you must do.

1) Receive Permission to burn. 2) Have an adequate water supply to control/extinguish the fire at all times. 3) All fires must be completely extinguished thirty minutes before sunset.

That next morning, I started out early heaping Ole Blue up with a load of scrap metal that even Fred Sanford would be proud of! I still have a couple more brush piles to burn,

but I can't burn anything until I have water to put out the fire should things get out of hand.

Mr. Kramer told me the windmill worked fine before the tail fin was folded in, and the mill was taken out of service. The tail fin is what guides the blades into the wind. The only reason I've been hauling water from town, is because I'm a chicken shit when it comes to heights. So far, I'd managed to put off the 60 foot climb.

I hauled scrap metal that day, and tried to keep my mind off the extra-large wind mill I knew that sooner or later, I'd have to muster the balls to climb.

Jazz circled the truckload of scrap that morning as I secured it to her satisfaction, then she hopped up in the passenger's seat, eager to hit the highway.

I'd raised her as a road dog from just a pup. By that time, she'd been with me over nine years. Together, we've played more bars than most people will ever set foot in.

We stopped in at 'County Line Liquor' to see Kory Katz, and get directions to the recycle center. Ole Blue was loaded up so tall, that I had to park by the road, and walk through the drive-thru.

"Mornin' Kory!" I say.

"Hauling junk today, are we?" "Yep!" Says I.

"Where'd it come from," She asked. "It's junk from the new property... I closed on the old Kramer place a few days back!"

"Well congratulations, Lefty!.. Are you still staying at Jeter Inn?" "Nope. I'm camped in the shade of my own oak trees."

"You had any company out there yet?" "Nope!" Says I.

"Good!" Says she. "I'm $50.00 short on rent this month. I hear there's a full moon tonight, want some company?" Kory asked mischievously. "No one enjoys a young woman's company like an old man Baby!" I say with a smirk.

"Do you think you can enjoy me fifty dollars' worth

tonight? I really need to pay that rent. I'd rather pay up in cash, so I don't have to pay up in ass!"

"Fifty is okay this time I say, but the last time you only charged me twenty dollars, Kory!" "Yea... she rebuts, but the time before that, I brought you a fifth of Jack Black, and didn't charge you a dime for the bottle or the sex! The time before that, you had me for the price of a song you ole Silver tongued devil!"

"Okay then, tell you what I'll do Kory... If you'll tell me where the recycle center is, and love me up tonight, I'll half that load with ya! Now, how's that sound?" "It's a deal!" Kory extends herself out the drive-thru window to seal the deal with a kiss.

"Stop on your way back, and I'll cash the check for ya. That way, I know I'll get mine," she says teasingly. "Oh you're gonna get yours Honey! Half the load today, and a full load tonight!" She scratches at me like a ravenous hell cat who can't wait to pounce. Her smile softens back to her usual sensuous grin, then gives me directions to the scrap metal yard.

Cory is the first woman I got to know in Jeter... Biblically speaking that is. She was a one-night stand that has lasted like a real relationship is supposed to, I guess? I don't know much about real relationships.

Being a traveling man, taught me might near everything a body could ever know about sex, but nothing about relationships, or what Kory Katz calls... "Intimacy."

Really getting to know people, is one of the best things about staying put. As for me and Kory? We'll never have anything more than a convenient arrangement to keep loneliness away from my doorstep, and the wolves away from hers, she's just too young for me.

On the way home from the recycle center, I stopped by "Mother Cluckers' Poultry Palace." I've never seen Kory when she wasn't hungry for fried chicken, and Mother Cluckers' was her favorite.

I waited my turn in line at "County Line Liquor," to cash the scrap metal check, and see Kory's eyes light up when she finds out I brought chicken. Kory holds up the check and inspects it with her big cat green eyes. She never blinks, unless she's flirting. "One Hundred Twenty-Six Dollars & Fifty Cents" she exclaims! "That's $63.25 each Lefty! I can make rent now" she says with a grin accompanied by a look of relief.

Kory is a pretty girl. Her Auburn hair hangs in ringlets that bounce just above her shoulders when she walks. Her skin is creamy chiffon with a delicate sprinkle of tiny freckles that arch her nose. Kory's eyes are translucent with shards of Amber, flecked with Emerald Green. They have a shine all their own, like something wild in the jungle.

There are women who look like they were plucked from Venus and planted on earth with but one single purpose... to please men. Pleasing men was something she was forced to do as a kid growing up under her grandpa's roof. He would trade her for moonshine mostly. As she grew into womanhood, giving favors to men just seemed to be her natural stock in trade.

In the course of a scandalous affair with State Representative C. Ray Wilson in Kansas City, Kory was exposed to the putrid stench of underhanded politicians, and high society's maggot ravaged underbelly. After all the 'Spin' had spun down, she longed for the simple life of a country girl and moved back home to Jeter.

Kory counted out my share of the scrap metal money, then glanced back at the after-work crowd that was steadily lining up behind me in the drive-thru. She ripped a huge chunk of chicken breast with her teeth, then stuffed a crush proof box of cowboy killers in my shirt pocket. "See you at your new place when I get off!" "K Babe!" Says I. Kory blows me a kiss through chicken packed cheeks as I drive away.

The moon was full that night, just as Kory said it would be. I set on the front porch steps looking over toward where the old railway station used to be. The windmill stood stark and foreboding in the silver moonlight between myself and the wooden water tanks that had somehow escaped demolition.

In the moonlight, I could see the rail bed rise above the tangle of brush and briers that had overtaken the old station. The tracks curved in from the main line, where the demolition crew manipulated the switch track plate, and came in with a flurry of men and machinery.

They made quick work of the roughhewn lumber that had stood the test of time, only to be hauled away on two flat cars stacked tall and bulging with everything but the concrete foundation.

I'd walked the place out only a few days before the

demolition crew showed up. Even though I'm not one who believes in ghosts, the old train station seemed spooky. Being a songwriter and all, I do pick up on vibes when they linger like unsung heroes in their long suffering.

Larceny can get the best of most any man, just as curiosity can. Especially when need becomes its own justification. After seeing a total lack of reverence by the crew in regard to the dilapidated old depot. And after considering that I had plenty of firewood, but no stove in which to burn it, I slipped over in the cover of darkness when the crew left, and tipped the ancient stove up in the bed of Ole Blue. I stashed it in the lawnmower shed until first frost. After a fresh coat of stove blacking and new pipe, the antique stove made the short list on my most prized possessions.

As I set on the porch steps fevorishly gawking up at the monster mill I was sure was out to emasculate me, I heard the sound of someone coming up the pasture road; it was Kory Katz. Her Jeep sounded just exactly like what it was... a Jeep. The Jeep was all she had managed to escape with from the scandal in Kansas City. There were a few grainy pictures published in the tabloids, but Kory had a home video that would ruin her Sugar Daddy's political aspirations without a doubt, not to mention his marriage.

Irrefutable evidence that would stand up in divorce court, and would give his wife the upper hand in the division of property. The secret video was her... 'Ace in the hole.' She used it without reprehension, as was her usual proclivity. It also kept her estranged lover abated.

With a clear title to the Jeep in hand, the Grand Cherokee brought her back home to Jeter in Grand style!

"Oh, how well I do remember this place! Kory exclaimed on her arrival. I learned to swim in those tanks!" She said, while pointing at the wooden casks that shone in the moonlight.

"Gramps used to deliver moonshine to the field hands out here. That was back before he got busted for making shine.

She paused and looked down at her feet. After that is when he started trading me for moonshine." She divulged timidly.

Kory stood silent while shaking off the memory, then sprang to life. "C'mon... let's climb the windmill!"

She lit out in just less than a full run like a kid headed for the monkey bars. Kory grabbed hold of the narrow steel ladder and raced up the rungs like she'd scaled the mill a thousand times before. Later that evening, after all the stories she told about the windmill, I discovered that my estimation of a thousand trips up the old windmill wasn't nearly the exaggeration I thought it to be initially.

The mill sported three landings. The first one about 20 feet up, it was the largest.

The other two landings were also about 20 feet higher

than the last. Each landing grew progressively smaller toward the top.

Kory stepped off the ladder onto the first landing. She looked down and found my eyes in awe of her. She crossed her arms with her elbows up high, and with one fell swoop Kory pulled off her halter top. Then she smiled a big sultry smile and said... "Come on up 'Big Boy'... but only if you want a blow job!"

After her ascent to the second landing, she threw her flip flops down at me. "C'mon Lefty! You aren't chicken... are ya'?" "No!" I say, trying to stave off the humiliation of it all. "I'm just hungry! You got any of that chicken left?"

"Nope!" Kory said holding her hands under her armpits like chicken wings. "You're the only chicken on the place!" She mocked me relentlessly while strutting around in circles and flapping her arms. Then she started clucking... It was more than my pride could take!

"All right then damn it!" I shouted at a dead run. You're fixin' to get fucked on that windmill woman!" "Won't be the first time!" She shouted back sarcastically.

As I made the first landing, I heard a loud squeak. Shrill, like fingernails on a chalkboard. Then came a loud hard snap! It sat up a vibration that traveled all the way down the windmill legs like an earthquake. It was all I could do to keep from screaming like a girl!

Kory had pulled the lock down lever that loosed the tail fin. I held fast to the ladder leading up to the second platform immobilized by fear. Kory let out an excited squeal as the tail fin caught a breeze and swung the huge fan into the wind. Looking up in amazement, I ascended to the second landing. I stared in awe at the sheer size of the water pumping monster's fan.

As the blades began to spin, the transmission set up a low moan howl, and the sucker rod began making long powerful strokes in and out of mother earth like a mechanical porn star! Before long we could hear water gurgling up the supply line and splashing into the big wooden tank.

That night I listened to a myriad of memories Kory told about the old train depot, and how it was haunted. She talked of the water tanks she learned to swim in. She spoke about picking up chunks of coal along the tracks with Gramps in Winter to heat the shanty. About flattening pennies on the train tracks.

She told about her high school days, and how the windmill was a favorite spot for teens to make out. Stories from back when she was one of the few girls in junior high who would... "go all the way." One thing about Kory, there's never been any shame in her game! To the best of my recollection, I've never had better sex than I did that night on the windmill with Kory. We saw the sun rise in all its glory that next morning. That night, we made love more times than a man of my age should be allowed by law!

By late that afternoon, the tank that still held water

was full. We swam in the cold clear water, and started all over again.

The old windmill has been pumping an endless supply of the freshest, coldest water I think I've ever drank. The blades turn when there isn't enough breeze to float the clouds, or so it seems. I haven't seen the blade come to a complete stop more than a dozen times since Kory scampered to the top of the mill and set the big blades to spinning. That's been almost three years ago now.

Every Spring I climb the tower and pump her bearings full of grease. My truck patch thrives on the perfect seven pH balanced water the old mill pumps to it. It keeps the one wooden tank that still holds water brim full.

I don't see Kory much anymore. She moved in with me the first year I bought the property. Her landlord kicked her out early in December of that year. I hadn't had a Christmas tree since I left home as a teenager. It was glorious!

We hung stockings on a makeshift mantel and strung mistletoe. Kory found a well-worn wreath at Good Will that looked like new when she hung it on the front door. We exchanged gifts that we both wrapped secretly. Both of us knew when a new gift had been placed beneath the tree by the conspiratorial smile that always accompanied it. Even Jazzy had something under the tree, and a stocking filled with squeeze toys and treats.

That first year abounded in joy. Kory filled my days

with laughter, and my nights with her softness. I'd never been happier! I loved Kory so much that I let her go. She was much too young and pretty to be my widow. We split the sheets, but parted friends.

When Kory showed up in the Summertime, we'd still swim in the big wooden tank, "Petty Coat Junction Style." (In the Buff) ... just like we have since the tank first filled, and just like she had from childhood.

"All the Lonely People... Where do they all come from?" That's a question the Beatles ask in the form of a song way back in the 1960's... I don't think anyone has ever found the answer... I've lived my life on a band stand looking out over a sea of cowboy hats, and the answer still alludes me.

We got an early warm rain last Spring. That gave us an early first cutting. We were finished with our second cutting by the first week in July. It was a good one too! We averaged 54 bushels per acre, and Mr. Kramer cultivates three sections.

Wheat is running about average on the commodities market, but we're going to get a bonus cutting this year. Mr. Kramer says If we can beat first frost, we should all be setting pretty this Winter. My money from the bonus cutting will put me ahead on the land payments. Security has become important to me.

A musician's life is the night life. "The Night Life, ain't no good life, but it's my life."

"Thank you, Willie Nelson!"

I remember a time when punching a time clock, was for other folks. The... 'work a day world,' was something I lived around, but never took part in.

I was 'different.' I had calluses on the tips of my fingers, not the course of my hands.

My work could not be covered up with a little dab of pookie, and another coat of paint. My work cannot be ground down, and re-welded. My work is music. There are no second chances. It's either right... or it sounds like shit for eternity!

Back in the day, when music was my only source of income, my day would generally begin like everyone else's ... with coffee. No matter where my day began, or what town I was in, it always started with tuning my guitar after coffee, and preparing for that night's gig.

For the first 20 years or so, that's how it went. After I began to age above 40, I didn't need as much sleep, so I began to rise earlier. I rarely miss sunrise these days. Back in the day, I was lucky to be up in time to catch a sunset.

Tomorrow, I have to be at Jeter Cafe around 5:30 a.m. to meet with the crew for this season's final harvest, but I don't need an alarm clock anymore.

Time changes all things, even if you don't want it too. In my shallow sleep, I'll hear the final bumper music playing when Coast to Coast goes off the air at 4 a.m. I'll brew a pot with an extra scoop of coffee in it, then I'll let Jazzy out to do her duty.

I always set patiently on the back steps while she squats, then sniffs around some. I've become more cautious in my old age, and won't take the chance of leaving her outside alone. I've lost a few chickens lately. Could be foxes, could be coons. At any rate, Jazz is a light weight, and I'd sure hate to lose her!

I pack a light lunch for myself while sipping coffee. I make sure Jazzy's water bowl is full, and fill her food bowl so she has a good lunch too. Then I'll hop in my faithful pick up, and head towards town.

Ole Blue has been a good truck for the most part. He's never left me by the side of the road. I've rolled the odometer over on him twice now. When I bought Ole Blue, he was actually, Blue.

I used to make a Winter circuit that took me all the way north to Manitoba. Them Ca-nooks sure do love themselves some Country Music! Canadian people are as nice as pie... they tip good too... like that money is fixin' to burn a hole in their pockets! Everyone in Canada has free healthcare. I guess that's why the women are so plump and tasty looking, with the prettiest teeth you ever saw!

I like the folks up north just fine. But my ole bones can't stand the cold anymore, and Ole Blue has had more than his fair share of road salt. Ole Blue? He still starts every time, and his heart is true Blue... even though now, he's rust colored mostly.

CHAPTER
SIX

I pulled up at Jeter Cafe in plenty of time for another cup of coffee, and one of the cinnamon rolls Jeter Cafe is famous for. They're almost as big as a dinner plate, and they draw cops, like moths to a flame.

I'd beaten everyone to the cafe except for ole Ben Hoover. His heavy-duty army issue bicycle was parked up in the bushes by the plate glass window where he could keep an eye on it. I've never met anyone like Ben Hoover. No Sir... never in all my born days!

They say a picture is worth a thousand words... If I could show you a picture of Hoover, it would save me at least a thousand words in the process of trying to explain this character! Trying to describe this fried chicken eating, foul smelling mountain of a man, would put any teller of tall tales to task!

Now ole Ben Hoover... he plays himself off as a good

Christian feller. And I ain't saying he ain't. I hear he's right there in the first-row pew every Sunday morning, rain or shine! Ben's wife is about five foot tall, and about five foot wide. After he and his wife joined the church, there wasn't enough room left on the first-row pew for the choir to set, so they moved on over with the Deacons and the Preacher's wife.

Now even though Ben and his wife profess to love the Lord without question, neither of them smell like it! About every other month or so, the Pastor preaches a sermon specially designed so he can slip that passage from the Bible in, the one that reads: "Cleanliness is next to Godliness."

I'm not much of a Church goer, but I hear tell from those who do attend regular, that their pew takes on a phew of its own every Sunday morning, I guess the Hoover's just don't catch it when the preacher likens cleanliness to Godliness.

Ben is a hard worker though. He trims trees when he's not trucking grain to the mill for Mr. Kramer during harvest. Most times he can be seen around town on a 40-foot ladder cutting branches with a pole saw. Actually, he's hard to miss at the top of an over loaded aluminum ladder.

That ladder bends like it's fixing to break with every pole saw stroke. It scares me to watch him working up high like that, on a ladder that was never designed to hold that much weight!

You would think a man of his stature would control everything in his world, but he don't. His wife wears the pants in that family, and there ain't no doubt about that.

She'll walk right up and tell ya,' that Hoover can out work any three men in the state of Kansas, then turn around and lick'em all three at the same time! I choose to believe her! One thing I'm sure of... I'd hate to be the man who begs to differ!

Ole Hoover likes me some. He says that my voice is as big as his arms. Even though he's so misogynistic that he pays himself a compliment the same time he pays me one, I still take it as a compliment, because his arms are huge... and his legs are like tree stumps! Ole Hoover don't have an ounce of fat on him anywhere. I guess that's why he dresses like Tarzan when he swings in the trees with his pole saw.

Even though his intelligence quotient may be teetering somewhere between 50 and 60 points in my estimation... the man is most definitely... Super-Sized! We're talking Biblical proportions here folks! This will be the fourth year I've worked with ole Ben.

It's comical to see him show up to the field riding in the truck bed. The Hoover's drive an old DATSUN mini truck from the late 70's. Hoover's wife drives the old DATSUN. Ben don't drive the DATSUN not because he can't drive, but because he's too large to fit in the cab. When he's not riding his super-sized expeditor bike from world war two, he rides in the truck's bed. The old

DATSUN is known as the "Arkansas Chug-A-Lug," among the locals.

The first time I ever saw the old DATSUN, was up on Town Square. It was running on three of its four cylinders… puttering along with a freak show sized man riding in the truck bed… that was Hoover.

Mrs. Hoover brings Ben's lunch to the field when he's working. She pulls up and drops down the tailgate and waits till Hoover makes another round in his grain truck. Then with her hands cupped around her mouth she hollers, "Hoovverrrr!" She pulls out a big red hand basket that conspicuously says, "DOLLAR GENERAL" on both sides. When she pulls back the grease-stained towel, it's always heaped up with enough fried chicken to supply a Baptist Preacher's Convention.

"Good morning, Hoover!" I say while making my way to the 12 top corner table, where the crew always meets. As I walk up, I see that there are already four big oval platters with enough pancake syrup left on them, to tell me he's already had four triple stacks of pancakes.

Hoover stands to shake my hand. My hand fits in his, like a link sausage in a foot long hot dog bun. "I won't grip you down this time Lefty, I know them there's, "guitar pickin' fingers!"

Just when I thought he'd paid me a compliment without his own self-aggrandizement included, he says: "I don't know how you get by with them tootsie roll fingers, I'd have a hard time pickin' my nose with one of them little suckers!

In the past I'd bitten my tongue more than a few times over this misogynistic asshole's total lack of respect for myself, and everyone else! Before I'd had time to consider the likely outcome of my actions, I balled up all my tootsie roll fingers into a white knuckled fist and threw a left hook that landed hard enough to send blood flying from the big ogre's potato sized nose!

He pushed the 12 top so hard that it sent chairs flying like they were bowling pins... then he turned the table over like they do in a John Wayne movie when someone gets caught cheating at poker...

I laid there on the red commercial carpet knowing for certain that popping ole Hoover had drawn me Aces & Eights... a dead man's hand!

Hoover grabbed up the 12 top table and held it over his head while he glowered down at me. He was just about to crush me like a bug, when four State Troopers bum rushed his ass! Three of them were on him like stink on shit, while the fourth Trooper held my head down with his knee and slapped on handcuffs.

The 12 top had taken two Troopers out of the fight. The Trooper that was still standing, looked like he'd just stumbled off a Merry Poppins movie set! My hands were cuffed behind me, so if ole Hoover whooped all four of them... (and he was mad enough too!) I knew for certain I was totally screwed! All I could do with the cuffs on, was to flop on my belly like a fish... so I did!

By this time, the whole restaurant was on their feet either headed for the door, or shooting video with their cell phones. The Trooper who had cuffed me took a backhand that knocked him cold as a wedge. That's when the percussion of a 38 Police Special rang everyone's ears... Hoover went down. The Sheriff showed up and took me downtown,

but not before the ambulance carted Hoover off to the hospital.

The Courthouse with its pillars of justice has a jailhouse underneath it that I didn't know existed until that day. I got a top-notch tour of the whole facility. First, I saw the booking room. The walls must have been white at one time. The paint had dulled to a color that I can only describe as Nicotine Beige.

There was a Formica countertop with bars that ran all the way across from wall to wall, except where the two pass-through windows were located. Behind the first window was a large bald-headed man who pushed a property basket through the window. He instructed me to take off my belt and put it in the basket along with any other possessions I had on my person. Then he made a list of everything in the basket. My billfold, pocketknife, car keys, and my cowboy killers, and my belt. He asked if that was everything I had on my person. I said that it was.

Then he signed at the top of the card, and I signed at the bottom.

Sheriff Gilbreth walked me to the second window where Baldy took my fingerprints, then handed me a slate with my name, and a number on it. Then he took my picture. Sheriff Gilbreth patted me down for a second time, then turned me over to the jailer.

"Well by God Lefty... I knew one day I'd hear you on the radio! I thought it would be

K-BOB Country. I Never figured I'd hear you on the police scanner, but there you was, first thing dis monin'! He laughed. How in da Hell did you piss Ole Hoover off so? Dat's what I wanna know, Lefty?"

"Well Marvin, says I. I told Hoover he was getting' fat! Now we both know there ain't an ounce of truth in that... I was just funnin' with him, but he took me serious! If it hadn't been for those K.H.P. Troopers, that son of a bitch would have killed me!"

Marvin Gott, is a big Black Dude that works part time as a bouncer over at

"Dance-A-Go-Go." (We've shot the shit over a cold beer more than a few times.) "Well youse jes' follow me Lefty, I'll show you to the shower. Den we'll get you dressed out."

Marvin told me to strip down, so I did. Then he sprayed me with a pump-up sprayer. "What the Hell is that shit Marvin?" "Dat's D.D.T. , it's 'Bug Killah'... It's so's de prisoners don't bring in no head lice and such truck.

Now wash dat shit offen ya' in da' shower while I get ya some threads what'll let folks know you a jailbird, should you try to fly da coup."

(Marvin's got some big White teeth that are fairly shinin' with his shit eatin' grin.) Marvin came back with a towel that looks the same color as the booking room walls... Nicotine Beige.

I scrubbed my head with the towel, then tried to cover my modesty, even though it was a little late for modesty!

"I had you figured hung like a stud horse Lefty! Marvin chuckled. He slaps his hands together and bends over laughing. Dem bitches dey been lying they ass off 'bout you boy!"

Not willing to take the jab, I says to Marvin. "I give women an engineer's rule when they measure Ole Porky. An engineer's rule is laid out in centimeters. The metric system, you know? It ain't long till what they think is10 inches shows up on an engineer's rule. Guess the joke's on them... while I'm shootin' my fun gun!"

I had the last laugh up until I put on a bright yellow jump suit with black stripes that ran horizontally. In the polished chrome mirror that distorts everything like a "Funhouse." My reflection looked like a human shaped bumble bee!

"Welcome home Lefty." Marvin says holding the cell door open for me. "I won't be in here long" I say. "I hope not, but don't hold your breath, Lefty!" Marvin slides the cell door closed and turns the key.

"Court is in cession every mownan at ten a.m. . Dat's about three hours from now. The docket may be full. If it is, then you'll see dee Judge tomorrow. May as well go on and make yourself comfortable, Lefty.

There were four cells, and only one other prisoner, so I got a cell all to myself. I was sure glad too! The other prisoner's eyes looked like they could cut through steel. His cell was covered in shit! He sat on the edge of his bunk working one arm against the other arm. Then that arm against the other.

Isometrics is what prisoners do when they're locked down to stay buff. The shit on his walls told me he was crazy. His stove pipe arms told me he'd been locked down all his life!

I'd been in jail a few times before, but always something petty. Busking on a street corner without a solicitor's license. Open container on a public beach. Insignificant stuff that didn't make a hill of beans.

Once I met this chick at Mar-Di Gras who was sharing a motel room with her brother. It was consensual sex, she wanted it bad as me! The brother was highly pissed and called the law anyway.

Marvin brought my lunch tray at noon. It wasn't Aunt Bee's jailhouse cookin,' like Otis used to get, but it wern't bad. I never got my king sized cinnamon roll at Jeter Cafe this morning, and I was sure enough due for something in my gut. Marvin served the crazy guy first, then he brought me my tray.

"Guess de docket was full today, Lefty," says Marvin. "I was waiting for da bailiff to calls yo' name, but he never dasent. Dat's okay, you be seein' de Judge nex monin'. I knowed cause I seed yo' paperwork. Da jes got you fo resistin' arress. Dat's just so's da can hold ya while detectives gets a low down on de ho story. If day don't throw it slap outta court, day'll least ways set a bond so's you can go yoself on home.

"Thanks Marvin. Mr. Kramer will go my bail. I'm surprised I haven't already heard from him, but today is the first day of our last harvest for the year, so I guess he can't get away just yet."

"Dat der Mr. Kramer… he's a goodern Lefty. He won't leave ya' up in here no mo longer dan what's a muss. My Pappy knowed him mose all his life, and spoke right smart 'bout that ole gentleman.

After I finished talking to Marvin and eating lunch, I laid down on my bunk and tried to sleep a little time off. Just as I was about to doze, the afternoon jailer came in with a garden hose and four big cops behind him. Then a small cop followed them in with a

12-gage shotgun.

The crazy Black dude just kept right on working his arms, one against the other. When he heard the keys rattling in the cell door, he flew up off his bunk, and went straight for the first cop that tried beating him down with his night stick. The other three rushed into the cell with their night sticks flying! I saw one cop go down and the cop with the shotgun draw a bead on the crazy man with the barrel of his gun through the bars. Finally, they got the crazy dude in handcuffs and leg irons. All four cops were bloody. It was hard to tell whether the blood was their own, or the crazy Black dude's. I've never seen such a beatdown!

The jailer turned the spicket and washed the shit off the walls while the small cop who had taken no punches, squeegeed all the shit down the floor drain. When the wash down was complete, the small cop picked his gun back up while the other four cops removed the crazy man's restraints and hauled ass before the crazy Black dude could get to them again. That crazy bastard was pounding the walls with his bare fists and foaming at his bloody mouth like a rabid dog when they left.

I pulled the covers up over my head and tried to put the bloody assault I'd just witnessed out of my head. When everything got quiet, I lay on my bunk for the first time since my incarceration, worrying about just how much trouble I might actually be in?

After I had settled some, the second shift jailer rattled his keys and said. "C'mon Fishburne, you have a visitor." He unlocked the door and led me through the facility to the visitor's room. Their set Mr. Kramer, and boy was I glad to see him!

"Are you okay, Lefty?" He asked with a genuine tone of concern. "Yes Sir, but I'm sure ready to be the Hell out of here!" "I bet you are Son. Now set down and tell me just how all this happened."

"Well Mr. Kramer, do you want to know what really happened, or do you want me to tell you what I told the cops?" "I wanna' hear both stories," he said with a tone of authority. So, I began from the beginning. When I'd finally finished telling him what happened, Mr. Kramer wanted me to reaffirm one point. "So… you actually hit that big bastard?" I shook my head solemnly in affirmation. "Damn, Lefty… you sure got some balls! I know a hundred men including myself, who have wanted to deck ole Hoover, but you're the only one I ever heard tell of, who actually did it!"

Mr. Kramer leaned a little closer and spoke. "What did you tell the cops?" "I just told them that Hoover had already eaten four platters of pancakes, and that I teased him about getting fat. Everyone knows you couldn't pinch an inch on ole Hoover. He's all bone and muscle… There ain't an ounce of fat on him. I told them that I was only teasing Hoover."

Mr. Kramer stood up and walked over to the Coke machine and asked did I want one too? I said I did, so he brought two back to his chair.

"I have some really good news, and some advice that might be a little sketchy, but I know it's what I would do if I was you, Lefty." "What's that?" I asked.

"Well, first of all I was parked next to your truck in the parking lot this morning when the Sheriff hauled you away. I didn't get there in time to see the ambulance, so I had no idea what had happened until I went in.

When I saw the back dining room turned upside down, I asked Vic. You know Vic the owner, right?" "Yeah, I know Vic" says I… Mr. Kramer continued. "Once I got the low down, I asked Vic if we could view the security camera tape.

On our way back to his office, Vic says, "Ole Sarge, my third shift dishwasher? He sleeps back at that corner table when things are slow. When he does, he moves the camera with his mop handle just enough that no one can see him sleeping on the monitor. He worked last night, so I doubt there's anything to see."

As Vic unlocked the office door, he explained further. "I'd fire anyone else, but he's been with me dang near 14 years. It's hard to keep a dishwasher for more than a month or two around here. He does me a good job, so I give him a pass on a little cat nap when it's slow."

"Lefty, Mr. Kramer said as he started to laugh in spite of himself. "The first time you showed up on the security camera was when you was floppin' like a fish on your belly with your hands cuffed behind your back. When the Sheriff stood you up and turned you around, your eyes were as big as the cinnamon rolls they serve at Jeter Cafe!"

We both laughed hardily, then Mr. Kramer leaned in close and said... "Now Lefty... here's what I'd do if I were you."

"The county detectives viewed the security tape after I'd already seen it, and there is no proof against you. It doesn't show you popping Hoover in his nose, or resisting arrest either. If I was you, I'd stick to what you told the cops, Son. That's exactly what I would do if I were you, Lefty! Fickle as ole Hoover is... no one will have a problem believing you either." "If that's what you say do… then that's exactly what I will do, Sir."

"Mr. Kramer... Hoover ain't dead, is he?" "No Lefty, he'll be laid up for a good long while though. They shot him in his knee cap... bone fragments all over the carpet...quite a mess it was! Serves the old cantankerous bastard right, far as I can see!"

Mr. Kramer motioned for the guard after we finished our Cokes... "Now you get yourself a good night's sleep Lefty. We'll be racing against a cold front on this last cut. You'll be harvesting wheat by the light of the moon come tomorrow night." "Sounds good to me Sir!"

"Mr. Kramer... can I ask a favor?" "What can I do?" "Can you stop by the house and feed my dog for me?" "Ole Jazz? No problem, Son! Now... get yourself some rest."

The guard escorted Mr. Kramer and I, back down the hallway toward the booking room. Mr. Kramer departed down a hallway marked: "VISITORS ONLY:" He turned and waved... "See you tomorrow!"

I went back to the booking room where they patted me down again, then the guard walked me back to my cell where he slid the door open, then closed it behind me.

I laid on the bunk and thought about how nice it would be to have this fiasco in the rear-view mirror. I thought about all Mr. Kramer had told me. I felt a little proud of myself for defending my own honor. I couldn't help but smile when I thought about all the "Adda Boy's" and pats on the back I knew would soon be forthcoming.

I thought about all the charges Hoover was facing for whipping four cops. The state don't take too kindly to whooping up on a Highway Patrolmen... much less four of them! Hoover will more than likely spend a stretch in Leavenworth, bad knee and all.

I folded my hands in prayer that night for the first time in a long while. I asked the Lord to forgive me for the lie I had conjured to try and keep my ass out of trouble. I asked forgiveness in advance for the lie I was fixin' to tell the Judge tomorrow. I don't know if it helped or not, but it eased me enough to sleep anyway.

"Fishburne!... Chow time!" It was Marvin Gott sporting his big toothy grin.

"Boy, you done got 'dis ho' town a jabberin'! Ya' ain't never heared sich da' like! Las I heared, you done whopped ole Hoover, den ya' done shot dat sucka! Said you done blowed dat dude's leg plum off!"

Marvin was laughing so hard; he nearly dropped my breakfast tray before he could slide it through the slot in the jailhouse door. We both laughed, then he continued!

"Dem gals gonna' be easy pickenz fo ya now Boy... Youz a Hero!"

Marvin reared back like a rubber band man and waved his hands in the air like a teenage girl at a reggae concert. When he came back to himself, He reminded me that he'd be back to take me to see the judge around 10 a.m.

Marvin walked back toward the hallway, then he spun and struck a pose like a gun<u>slinger</u>. His knees were bent, with both hands pointed at me like he was holding pistols... "Dat is... if youz ain't too busy signing autographs!

Marvin broke out yet again in a fit of laughter. His knees bent, and his hands went down to his crotch like he was fixin' to pee himself. He finally turned back toward the hall still convulsing with laughter... I could hear him laughing all the way to the booking room.

I avoided looking over at the crazy Black dude's cell until after I'd finished my breakfast. There might be shit on the walls again this morning. Just as I washed down my last bite of scrambled eggs with a sip of coffee, yesterday's crew of Deputies showed up again, including the small guy with the big shotgun.

It was obvious to me that the crazy Black dude had landed his fair share of punches yesterday. No one had gone unscathed, except for the small Deputy with the big shotgun.

The crazy Black dude was setting on the edge of his

bunk with his elbow perched on his knee, working one arm against the other. He was glistening with a lather of sweat. When he heard the jailer's key slip in the steel door, he launched himself off the bunk. When he landed, his back was arched like a Black cat! His massive shoulders rippled with anticipation. His big guns were fully loaded and ready to land a punch. He was ready to do battle!

Just when I knew for certain I was about to witness another beatdown, a lady in a nurse's uniform walked up to his cage and asked in a soft, but firm voice. "Cedric... are you ready to go home?" The crazy Black dude turned in her general direction. There was no possible way he could see through those painfully swollen eyes! "Cedric... are you ready to go home?" She repeated, in a soft comforting voice. "This is Nurse Murphy... are you ready to go home?" She asked for a third time.

The crazy dude said something that was indistinguishable to my ears that was coming from his pulverized mouth, but evidently, she understood. "Yes... this is Nurse Murphy," was her reply. Cedric's shoulders slumped, and his head hung low in an obvious show of relief... then he began to weep.

As the crazy dude stood crying submissively, Nurse Murphy glared with indignation at each of the deputies who by their own bumps and bruises, gave testimony to participation in the horrific state of disrepair they'd left Cedric's face in. She was seething!

"Any one of you man enough to go in there by yourself?... No takers?... Any two of you? She persisted. I thought not!"

All four deputies shrunk like shrinking Violets... Then she turned to the little deputy with the big gun. "Hey Small Fry, you got handcuffs?" He produced a pair. "Come with me!" she commanded.

"You... take the shotgun big guy!" She instructed the deputy who had probably dealt out the most licks from yesterday's beating. His face and the cast on his arm bore witness to the fact that he had obviously taken the most.

"Open the door jailer." The door opens... she steps in... "Bring your cuffs and come on in deputy." Ever so hesitantly, and only after the little guy sees the shotgun pointed at the crazy Black dude's head, he cautiously steps in the cell. "Cedric, we need to put cuffs on. I won't let anyone hurt you. This man with the handcuffs has never hurt you... Put your hands behind you Cedric."

Nurse Murphy gently squeezed both the crazy Black dude's hands with her own. He leaned against the wall peacefully and did as he was instructed.

Side by side the nurse walked her patient out the jail door and down the hall with the 12 gauge still trained at the back of the prisoner's head. I'd never seen such shit as that!... Not even on TV!

Time rolled slow as penitentiary time generally does... or so I'm told. I ain't never been in no serious trouble, so I ain't done no 'hard time.' But I've heard that from those who have.

They say that every minute behind bars, feels like an hour in your street clothes, and I believe every word of it! I remember what my grandma always said… a watched pot never boils.

I stretched out on my bunk relieved to know that ole Cedric was headed back to the loony bin. I was even more relieved to know that he hadn't shit the place up before he left.

I pulled the covers over my head and practiced holding my eyes open. I've always heard that when a person is lying, they blink their eyes a lot. I knew the Judge that would soon be sizing me up, had been lied to a lot in his line of work, so I practiced telling my lie without blinking.

When I figured I had it down pat, or as good as I could, without my eyeballs falling out, I closed my eyes and rested.

Next thing I know, there was Marvin. "Fishburne! Front and cenna, you due to see da Judge… Judge Harris!" I sprung to my feet in a quickness. "Judge Harris? I say. You mean the one everyone calls the, 'Hanging Judge?" Dat's right Boy! I've seen hem throw 90 days at a Nigga for spittin' on da sidewalk… iffin' he tanks dat Nigga be lyin!"

I appropriate his Ebonics dialect long enough to axe a

question like a brotha. "You wouldn't lie to a Nigga der would ya Mer Marvin?" "Yeah I'd lie to a Nigga iffin he be my own homeboy, or iffin he wern't... but don't you be frettin' none Lefty. I done seen you wit out yo' drawers! I don't know what you is Boy... but you damn sure ain't no Nigga!"

We both busted out laughing. I had no choice but to take the jab that time! He turned his key, and I was on my way to court.

Like Town Square, the courtroom was not square at all. The walls curved and the ceiling was arched like the Astro Dome. Everything was red stained Mahogany.

The bailiff received me at the double doors and showed me to a bench where I sat alone in my Yellow and Black Bumble Bee jumpsuit. I was the only prisoner in custody.

Men dressed in suits and ties scurried around in consultation with other men dressed in suits and ties as well. Mostly, people were dressed casually. The organized kayos persisted for a while. Then a well-rehearsed voice rose above the muffled tones and soft exclamations common to a courtroom before it comes in cession.

"All rise!... This court is now in session... The Honorable Judge John D. Harris presiding." "Good morning," the Judge greeted in a rather joyous tone, especially considering his reputation as, "The Hanging Judge." Everyone who hoped to be the benefactor of his good disposition returned his salutation with an equal amount of fervor.

Judge Harris glanced at what I assume to be the docket, then without further

a due, he turned to the bailiff and spoke. "Bring the prisoner forward please."

The bailiff motioned for me to come forward, so I did. "Please state your full name Sir." "Preston Augustus Fishburne Sir." The Judge pulled his glasses slightly toward his nose and looked over them as if to take a mental picture of me, then he addressed the prosecuting attorney by his Sir title.

"Mr. prosecutor, I have the name on this case number listed as Benjamin Hoover. The charges against this man before me seem rather doubtful considering they allege assault on four State Highway Patrol officers resulting in an altercation that required the use of deadly force. Judge Harris looked back at me and asked, Mr. Fishburne, have you been shot? "No Sir, it was Ben Hoover... he's the one who got shot."

The prosecuting attorney approached the bench holding a note handed him by the Deputy Sheriff who arrested me. "Mr. Fishburne, approach the bench please." So I did. "Mr. Fishburne, somewhere in the process, of the due process of law, mistakes are made from time to time. In review of the facts of this incident, it appears that you were the victim of this assault, not the aggressor. Is that correct?" "Yes, Your Honor."

"Mr. Fishburne, I would like to extend an apology on behalf of Jefferson County for the duress and inconveniences that were incurred by yourself and your family in your unjustified detainment. You will be compensated for any work you may have missed as well as any expenses you may have been assessed with that are directly related to your absence this clerical error has caused." "Thank you, your Honor!" I say. "Mr. Fishburne: Once again, the Judge reiterated, My sincere apologies...you are free to go Sir."

I turned away from the Judge and breathed a sigh of relief. I was free to go, and I didn't have to tell a lie under oath. Stealing a couple of screws from Chalmer's Hardware each fall is one thing, but lying directly in a Judge's face is a horse of a different color!

Unbeknownst to me, Mr. Kramer had entered the courtroom and was setting by the big double doors in the back. He stood and pushed the closest door open where I glided through without slowing my pace... he fell in behind me. "You couldn't ask for a better outcome than that Lefty... You're Scott free and didn't even have to lie!"

After changing out of my Bumble Bee suit and collecting my things from the property room, Mr. Kramer and I, stepped out into the first sunshine I'd seen in a couple of days. Even though the air was Autumn crisp, clouds from a northern direction lurked ominously with the promise of a radical change that was no longer a question of if, but rather of when.

CHAPTER

SEVEN

Mr. Kramer took me back to Jeter Cafe where Ole Blue still stood in his tracks, right where I'd left him. "Pack a good lunch and check on your dog. Meet me at the tractor shed at two p.m. I'll road you out to the field with the rest of the crew."

Mr. Kramer's voice had taken on a sense of urgency as he told me about the weather forecast predicting temperatures teetering around the freezing mark, with a second cold front sure to drop the bottom out!

Jazzy danced in circles on my arrival. I was as glad to see my ole singing dog as she was to see me! While I made a fresh pot of coffee and packed a heavy lunch, she stayed close at my feet. Jazzy had ridden on the combine before. Being as I was scheduled for a shift that would last the rest of the day all through the night, and possibly into the next day, I was bringing her along.

I packed enough ham in my lunch bucket to feed ole Jazz as well as myself. I filled my thermos jug with hot coffee, then Jazz and I, headed for Mr. Kramer's tractor shed.

"Watta' you think about her Lefty?" "She's a Bute Mr. Kramer!" He smiled with a look of adoration as he walked me around his new John Deere combine. "That's the

X9 1100 Series, Lefty. He announced proudly. She'll harvest 30 acres per hour on 20 percent less fuel. If we can get you roaded over to the field by four o'clock. You should have your section harvested by around four a.m. tomorrow morning."

I climbed aboard and fondled the leavers with delight... "Oh Man! I exclaimed... this is way better than that old Massey Ferguson you started me out on!" Mr. Kramer smiled when I turned the key and brought the new velvet monster to life. "You ready to go to work, Son?"

(Mr. Kramer turned 84 years old a few days before I met him at the Legion Hall.) It wasn't long after that he took me under his wing. Sometimes he calls me... "Son." I think it must be a fatherly instinct more than anything else. Regardless of why, it's not a bad thing to hear, since I'm past retirement age myself.)

I let the big diesel clatter while I grabbed my lunch and thermos bottle from Ole Blue. "Load up Jazz." Jazzy negotiated the steps and settled at my feet. "Let's gett'er done!" I say enthusiastically.

Mr. Kramer fell in behind the new John Deere with his pickup's emergency lights flashing. The new harvester roaded good, and of course… ran like a Deere!

Unlike the old Massey Ferguson I was used to operating, the new John Deere had a cab. There were knobs and switches everywhere. First thing off I found the radio, it had a full sound with lots of bass.

Even before the sun went down, the first cold front began to settle in my bones as I made round after round. After finding the appropriate knobs and switches, the cold was no longer a problem. The new 'Deere' had a heater.

It took a steady stream of grain trucks to keep up with the output of the new machine. The grain truck that was usually driven by Ben Hoover, was being driven by a tall thin woman with a long nose and jet-black hair.

Just about dawn the caravan of trucks and equipment made the final turn on the road back to where we started out from. Mr. Kramer swung open the double wide gate and pulled up by the tractor shed.

Through the night, a stiff northeast wind began to blow as the second front followed the first one in. Then a light rain turned to sleet just as I parked the new combine. There was already a layer of ice on Ole Blue's windshield by the time we got back to the tractor shed.

The truck drivers all turned in their paperwork from

the grain elevator. One by one, each driver got paid in cash. After a handshake with Mr. Kramer, they all lit out for home except for one... The lady who had driven Hoover's grain truck.

She was setting in a yellow Volkswagen. Strapped to the top of the V.W. was a single piece of luggage that looked like an Army issue footlocker.

Me and Jazz and Mr. Kramer set in his truck while he wrote me out a check for my wages instead of paying me cash. He folded the check on the perforated line in his checkbook, then ripped it out after he had noted his math on the attached receipt.

"I'm going to pay you in a check this time Lefty. That way you can take it to the Courthouse as proof of the wages lost while you were in the poky."

"That's a great idea Mr. Kramer. After they make a copy, I'll sign the check, and give it back to you toward what I owe on the property." "That's fine with me, Lefty."

I glanced down at the check, then looked again. "Four hundred and fifty Dollars is a lot of money for one night's work, Mr. Kramer," I exclaimed.

"Look at it like this Lefty; If you hadn't showed up to help me with harvest, you wouldn't have ended up in jail. Just figure your wages are for three days."

About that time there came a knock on the truck window. It was the tall woman with the black hair and long nose. Lester pushed the button on the driver door, and rolled down the passenger window.

"I just wanted to thank you again for the work, Mr. Kramer. That'll get me a long way toward Frisco in my V-Dub!" Said the mesmerizing Gypsie. Then she continued. "First, I need a shower and some rest before I hit the road again. Can you recommend a cheap motel?" Simultaneously, Mr. Kramer and I say in unison... "The Jeter Inn."

"Sounds good... where's it at?" She asks. "It's on my way home, follow me and I'll show you." I volunteer... all the while wondering if there might be a chance for a little romance in the bargain.

"Can we stop for some coffee and breakfast on the way? I'm starving!" She added. "That sounds good to me, says I. I'm ready for a good breakfast my own self!"

Of course this was an outright lie. Jazzy and I had polished off all but one of the ham sandwiches in my lunch bucket. We had both eaten until neither of us could hold another bite... even the coffee thermos had a splash left.

Eagerly, I shake Mr. Kramer's hand with a thank you, and open his pickup door. He can see I'm ready to beat a hasty retreat. "Go on now Lefty says Kramer... every man who ever got out of jail never has anything on his mind better than the touch of a woman." "Thank you, Sir!... Yes... you're right about that!"

Jazzy hopped to the ground headed for Ole Blue. The yellow Volkswagen pulls in behind me as I follow Mr. Kramer out the gate. Normally, I would get out and lock the gate, but this time Kramer pulls to the roadside and steps out to tend the gate. He knows what's up. He knows this old dog still hunts, so he waves me on by. I pull around his pickup and go on toward Jeter Café, with the Volkswagen close behind.

The defroster had melted the ice off my windshield, but sleet had begun to collect on the roadway. The weatherman's voice had pitched half an octave lower, as his weather forecast boomed through the truck radio. The voice he was using now, was the one he had rehearsed in the bathroom mirror all the way through meteorological school. It was not his usual 'Sunshine Voice,' but the well-rehearsed voice of impending doom.

Normally, the weatherman is just another familiar voice on the radio. Normally, he sounds like any other fair-weather friend you've ever had, right up until he turns on you!

The voice that usually floats like a feather on the breeze, now sounds ominous and foreboding.

"The National Weather Service has issued a hard freeze warning for Jefferson and surrounding counties. Officials urge residence to prepare for what some are calling,

(And I Quote:) "An unprecedented early Autumn storm." Stay tuned to K-BOB Country for information as it becomes available. Remember folks; bring your pets inside, dress in layers, and drip those pipes… it's gonna' be a cold one!"

Sand trucks were parked in rows at Jeter Cafe. Luckily, we both found a parking spot. The high banked curvy roads of Jeter's infrastructure have proven to be a challenge when Mother Nature comes calling in the inevitable reality of Winter. I think Mr. Rockwell was more concerned about the apple cheeked children having a place to sled, than how many trucks, and how much sand it would take to keep traffic moving. All and all, Winter snowstorms are just another chapter in our little story book town's history.

The hostess greeted us at the door. "Good morning, Lefty! Two for breakfast?" "Yes Mam… If you can find room for us?" I say rhetorically. "I'll put y'all in the Party Room. Looks like we're going to have to open it anyway." The Hostess leads us to the rear of the diner and pulls back a Red Velvet accordion style curtain. She seats us at a table by the front window where we watch the sleet turn to large flakes of snow. After handing each of us a menu she asks: "Two coffees?" "That sounds good Rita May!" Great! I'll be right back with a pot…

With the Hostess gone after coffee, my breakfast guest with Raven hair says to me. "It would be my guess that you know everyone's name in here except for mine. Is that right Lefty?" "Almost everyone's, I retort apologetically. Please forgive me… "My name is Preston, but everyone calls me Lefty." I lean forward and offer my hand, which she obliges. "My name is Esmeralda. Mr.

Kramer didn't mention me?" "No Mam." I've been a little… incapacitated lately."

"You mean incarcerated, don't you?" Esmeralda smirks. She tries to keep a straight face but can't. "Trust me, she elaborates, everyone at the Legion Hall was talking about you. They were calling you, "Jack the Giant Killer!" (Now we were both laughing.)

Evidently, we were laughing rather loudly because 'Sarge' jumped to his feet from behind the twelve-top where he was catching a catnap. Sarge immediately picked up a broom and dustpan. He made an obvious show of tidying up around the 12-top. He then arranged all four chairs he'd been sleeping on back to their proper places. Glancing over his shoulder at us, he departed through the red velvet accordion curtain. On his departure, he nonchalantly gave the surveillance camera a calculated tap with his broomstick.

"So… how did you end up in Jeter Kansas?" I asked with a genuine tone of curiosity.

"It's kind of a long story." She said, holding her head to one side. She obviously wasn't sure she wanted to confide in me. Noticing her hesitation, I tried to reassure her. "It couldn't be any weirder than the way I got here!" I said in effort to coax her story out.

"Yeah… I can just imagine how weird your arrival was," she says after a long moment's silence. "I can almost see the headline in the morning paper." She stares down her long nose at me and holds her hands above her head… using her fingers as quotation marks.

" LOSER MUSICIAN MAKES GOOD IN JETER KANSAS!"

Lost in what had just become a confrontational conversation, neither of us were aware that Rita May stood before us holding two cups, and a pot of coffee... "Here y'all go!" Rita May lands Esmeralda's cup in front of her, and fills it to the brim. Then she pours mine with a sort of circus show swirl... like my cup had been blessed with her own brand of magic.

She looks at me cock eyed trying to read the dumbfounded expression on my face. I roll my eyes to indicate I'm having a conversation with a person that may be a little off center. She reads me loud and clear.

After taking an assessment of the tall lady's indignant look, she glances back at me and nods in affirmation. Rita May opens her eyes wide. She stretches an artificial smile across her face as she announces... "Your waitress will be right with you."

I take a sip of my coffee and say to Esmeralda: "Why you wanna' judge me like that... I ain't done a damn thing to you!"

"You haven't yet, but I've dated musician's before!" She retaliated angrily." "Dated?... I asked, with my own anger showing now. Who the Hell ask you out anyway? I damn sure didn't! All I did was tell the boss that I'd show you where the Jeter Inn was!... Guess that's what I get for volunteering!"

She shrank back in her chair knowing I had gained the upper hand over her presumptuous assessment that we were on a date. Even though I had been victorious in making her look self-centered, I still felt my ears beginning to turn red, so I excused myself and headed toward the "Men's Room." "If the waitress comes while I'm gone, order me a cream cheese cinnamon roll... please!"

Walking past the counter through the main dining room, I could see people's faces aglow with the first Rosie cheeks that had come just a little early for some, and none too soon for others.

The Summer had been exceptionally hot, but had been punctuated with enough rain to make the season's harvest a bountiful one.

A few people hailed me to ask about what happened between Ben Hoover and me, but the vast majority of chatter was about the nor eastern that was dropping down on us from Canada.

By the time I'd made my way back to the party room, my cream cheese cinnamon roll sat oozing with its white cream frosting in a slick shiny glow. Butter slowly melted, making a Golden stream that divided itself into tributaries that trickled down the cinnamon coated swirls like a water slide only to puddle on the edge of my plate.

Esmeralda sat waiting for me patiently with her hands folded in her lap, even though her own food was getting cold. Her hateful countenance had been replaced with a measured look of trust, almost to the point of piety. Her lips now shown their fullness under a shimmering new coat of red lipstick. Her raven hair was parted in the middle and glistened as it flowed past her high cheek bones down past her shoulders almost to her waist. Without the encumbrances of her heavy coat and fur lined hat, her nose now looked proportionate to her face.

"Let's eat I say… rubbing my hands together while sliding into my side of the booth.

I hope your food didn't get cold?" I ask with a tone of apology. "Not at all… Your timing couldn't be more perfect!" she exclaimed, raising her coffee cup with her pinkie slightly crooked as a perfectly cordial lady would.

Esmeralda was by no means a perfectly cordial lady though. As I began to take in the full essence of her being, I could almost see the Gypsy blood pulsing through her flesh. She was no more a perfectly cordial lady than a timber wolf is a lap dog! Each time she sipped her coffee, her eyes would flash another facet of her inner darkness for me to behold.

I became ravenously aware of the erection she beguiled me with. As I fell deeper and deeper under her spell, the more amorous I became. The swelling in my pants became a tempestuous torture as she held my mind telepathically.

"STOP! She commanded while snapping her fingers... I was completely bewitched. Mesmerized by the Gipsy woman. "Not here, she said. There's time."

As our breakfast conversation took a turn for the better, the weather outside had taken a turn for the worst. "I lived at the Jeter Inn for a while back before I bought my property," I told her, while trying desperately to regain some semblance of control.

After all, she had practically raped me with her mind from across the table. "As long as there's plenty of hot water and a soft bed, I'll take it," she said softly.

"I never ran out of hot water when I was in room seven. Maybe you should try for Lucky Number 7… I got lucky there a few times!" I added jokingly.

I was trying to play it cool, and not succeeding. I'd heard of Sirens, and their song of the sea that has led many a sea fairing man to his doom. I think it a fair analogy that Gypsy's are to a traveling minstrel, what a Siren is to a sailor.

"Did you get enough to eat?" I asked while picking up the guest check. "I'll pay half that," she interjected referring to our breakfast tab. "You're traveling, hold on to your money, I got this! It's a long way to San Francisco." I said while helping her with her coat.

I paid the check, then led her through the double glass doors into the Winter wonderland that Jeter had become in the interim.

The fleet of sand trucks were all gone. Each of them

had left a tell tail trail behind them making passage for us easy, as we headed for Jeter Inn.

Upon arrival it was obvious that all the rooms had already been taken. The parking lot was packed all the way around the horseshoe shaped parking lot, and the sign flashed... "NO VACANCY."

She followed me in her Volkswagen to the guest registry awning where I got out of Ole Blue. She rolled down the Beetle Bug window and asked with the most forlorn look on her face... "What am I going to do now?"

Shortly thereafter, I began to feel my pants swell as she locked me in her eyes again. I was no longer in control. She conveyed to me through transcendental meditation just how this scenario was going to play out.

Part of me was afraid. That part wanted to jump back in Ole Blue and haul ass. Another part of me wanted to succumb to her sultry evil magic and experience her Hellish Heaven. Yet another part of me was deeply concerned about my Soul.

For a second time, she snapped me out of the trance with her fingers. When I had come back to myself, she smiled a devilish grin and said: "I'll follow you."

I slung Ole Blue back onto the slushy pavement behind a sand truck headed for the bridge, whose steel strands arch at the top of the world to remind all who traverse its span, that life's beauty can only be encompassed when self-imposed limitations are broken away, and overcome by the magical elixir of imagination and tenacity.

I made my way a few miles more, took a right across the railroad tracks, then turned down the road leading home. We were going slow on the un-plowed road with windshield wipers slapping hard at the snow.

The radio was rattling my speakers with the intensity of the weatherman's voice that had dropped even lower than it was on our way from the field. His tempo has slowed markedly, and his diction was impeccable. His tone was pure eloquence! Worthy of his metamorphosis from familiar radio voice to 'Weather God!'

Jazzy and I hadn't seen roads like this since our last northern tour through Canada. Just as she had done then, Jazzy had her paws on the dashboard helping me stay between the ditches.

CHAPTER

EIGHT

Driving down the pasture road to my house, I guessed my way through mostly. Everything looks different under a blanket of freshly fallen snow. There are only fence posts to judge where the road was until I could see the house.

The truck patch looked stark in the snow drifts that sloped up like a ski jump. The wire mesh tomato baskets were covered in a thick layer of ice. My black berry bushes stood in their arbors glistening.

I saw no tire tracks on the pasture road, no signs of human foot traffic either. Yet there was smoke swirling up from the new stove pipe! I assumed that a friend had stopped by to build a fire so my water pipes wouldn't freeze. Someone who thought I was still in the pokey I reckoned.

I parked next to the motor hoist I'd used to lift the

stove onto the porch. I try to put things back where they belong after I've finished using them. After the trip to see Dr. Fred at the chiropractor's office, then the run in with Ben Hoover, then going to jail, then getting in this year's last harvest by moonlight, then this God forsaken nor eastern blowing in, I hadn't had a chance to winterize. Even still, it was good to be home!

I step out into the blowing snow, happy in the thought that at least I'm stocked up on stove wood!" Jazz follows me out the driver door and sniffs at the snow like it's beneath her dignity to be bothered with it. Then she noses around and finds rabbit tracks leading down toward the chicken house. Evidently, we have a new resident rabbit.

"Is this your house?" asks Esmeralda. Lost in my own thoughts, I'd almost forgotten she'd come home with me. "This is it I say… home sweet home!"

You know you have a ghost… right?" "Honey, I'm too far out in the country to even get trick-or- treaters at Halloween!" I say laughing. "No seriously … she insists, you have a ghost!"

I kicked the snow away from the threshold and shake the snow off the screen door, then lead the way in, holding the door open for Esmeralda. She streaks across the living room floor and huddles next to the stove while cussing her Volkswagen heater… or lack thereof.

Esmeralda holds her hands over the stove soaking in the warmth. "He's in here... your ghost... He's inside your stove." She says looking directly at me and pointing her index finger straight at the stove top.

I open the stove door to see if I need to stoke the fire or load in some wood. I look all around the inside trying to keep a straight face. "I don't see no ghost in here. I don't see anything, but a couple chunks of coal."

Without further rebuttal she asked, "why do you have all that wood stacked against the wall if you burn coal?" "I don't burn coal!" I retort. "Well, somebody does!" she shot back.

Sure enough, I looked over behind the stove and saw a small coal bucket. It looked like an antique toy, but it was full of coal.

"I don't know about you Ghost Lady, but I'm ready for a shot of Jack Black... care to indulge?" "It's kind of early for me, but... what the Hell!"

The house was already warm as toast. I could tell the stove had already been hot enough to burn the blacking off the new stove pipe. The embers in its big cast iron belly, were all that remained from this very first fire of that season.

I usually burn the pipes off with all the doors and windows open, so I don't stink the place up. Whomever lit the stove must have followed my procedure, because not a waft of the pungent oily odor was detectable.

"Here ya' go Esmeralda. I handed her a double shot of Jack Black on the rocks.

Shoot that straight down to your belly button... that way you'll get the burn!"

"This place is nice and cozy!" She says, holding herself in a comfortable embrace. I take her remark as a compliment until she adds... "Does it have indoor plumbing?" I look at her cross eyed, then the corners of her mouth curl up into a smile. "Of course it does," says I. "I'll give you the grand tour." "That sounds great, she says with hesitation, but can you show me the bathroom first?"

"C'mon! I say, leading her from the living room down the hallway into the kitchen. I lead her through my bedroom into the bathroom. I showed her where the washcloths and towels were. "There's a laundry room just off the kitchen if you need to do a load." "I may take you up on that in the morning. Meanwhile, do you have some sweatpants and a warm shirt I can put on?" "Sure Ghost Lady!" (I flash a teasing look at her... she looks perturbed with me.)

"Make fun of me all you want... but only if you're willing to let me host a seance here tonight." "Sure! I say beaming with confidence, but only if we can top the night off with a good game of... "Spin The Bottle?" "Fine by me." She replies with a sultry smile.

Being the dick I am, and knowing a kiss has been all but promised, I go ahead and steal a little one... just as a sampler. That's when I realize she's half a head taller than I am. This turns me on some. After I taste her lips, I come down off my tip toes only to realize her titties are almost in my face. This turns me on even more!

In an effort to perpetuate the ghost in the stove joke, I tell her to check the commode before she squats. "I've never seen a ghost in the pot, but I did have a rat snake come up through the septic tank once." Yet again, she fails to find the humor in my sarcasm, so I pull the bathroom door closed and beat a hasty retreat and give her privacy.

I load the stove with firewood and turn the damper down, then I slip on my camo coat, and head out the back door to feed the chickens. When my girls are not in 'molt', I get a couple dozen big brown eggs from their nesting boxes most every morning. I can sell every egg Jazzy and I don't eat. We both like scrambled eggs. I get two dollars a dozen if you have your own carton, five dollars if you don't.

The chicken house has an automatic watering system that keeps them in all the fresh water they want. From plywood, I built a gravity fed feeder box that keeps them in all the crumbles they care to eat. Even though I've been in jail, they never missed a meal. On days when I work around the house, I turn them out in the truck patch to eat bugs and forage. Today is not one of those days. The girls huddle close together sharing body heat.

The wind cuts at me as I watch the snow that continues to pile in drifts. The power lines are drooping low and heavy with a thick layer of Ice. I can hear weighty tree limbs crackle under the strain of the accumulated ice and snow. Everything sparkles with the splendor of a Christmas card.

The windmill blades seem to have spun off every drop of rain before it had a chance to freeze. The huge snowflakes ride the turbulence through the front of the fan. When they come out on the backside, they've been sifted to a powder so fine they drift away on the breeze, like smoke from the chimney.

I've lost power out here in the middle of nowhere a few times before. The Rural Electric Cooperative seems to put my repairs off until last. The likelihood that limbs will break, and lines will fall is more than likely before this storm has passed.

For this reason, I slip a screwdriver from the hasp where a lock should be, and open the door on the lawnmower shed. On a shelf along the back wall beside my tacklebox, over in the corner with my fishing rods, sets another "find," from the old train station before Kansas City Southern sent in their demolition crew. An antique Brakeman's lantern.

It is solid Brass with an ancient coat of Grey Green patina. The globe looks like an old Ball Mason jar, except the glass is much thicker. I fill it to the brim from a faded kerosene can I assess to have been Fire Engine Red a few decades ago.

Looking at the can in bright sunlight, you can make out the words, 'Coal Oil'. I grab the lantern by its bail and swing it with pride as I make my way through the storm like many a brakeman has in the past.

There's a special feeling I get when carrying the old lantern. It's almost like an honor that has been passed down to me along with its possession. An honor that goes all the way back to the Spring of 1869, when the Golden spike was driven in celebration of the transcontinental railroad's completion.

Once inside the warm kitchen, I hang my coat on a nail driven behind the door for that very purpose. I see no sign of Esmeralda anywhere in the house, until I check the bedroom. She's lying sprawled out spread eagle on the bed without a stitch of clothes on.

Her hands are above her head, and her flat stomach rises and falls in a gentle way, like a very young child. Her course black mane flows so rich and pure along her slender body. It makes a flip, then pools like a puddle of ink, just above her waistline.

I've always liked women who shave themselves smooth along the length of their legs. Her legs as far as anyone could tell, have never felt the stroke of a razor. A flush of rich black foliage flourished from each arm pit. Her eyebrows arched high with the thickness of an Egyptian Princess. Her body hair was not course at all, but so delicately fine that my fingers longed a touch, but I dare not.

I left Esmeralda in her slumber and headed for the shower myself. I hadn't bathed since Marvin the jailer sprayed me down with D.D.T. in the bowels of Jeter's dungeon style jailhouse.

Even though cleanliness is next to Godliness for most folks, with the exception of Ben Hoover and his wife, along with the homeless, and a few musicians I've known, there was also another factor that even above Godliness, made me want to be squeaky clean.

The thought of crawling in the bed next to Esmeralda enticed me to polish certain extremities of my body more than others. One extremity in particular seemed to have precedence over the others and gravitated out toward my soapy hand.

I had previously laid Esmeralda out some sweatpants and a flannel shirt. She could have dressed in modest casual comfort before retiring for a nap, yet she chose to lay naked in my bed. I'd already made it perfectly clear to her that I had two bedrooms, but only one bed. Looking back now I see clearly... What she wanted, was to be ravaged!

I learned long ago that patience is a virtue. Somewhere along the gently arched learning curve of wisdom, I discovered why patience is so important. Quite simply, because timing is everything! Timing is so important in fact, that without patience, perfect timing is unattainable.

I felt a sharp pulsating release in the shower that assured me of two things simultaneously. 1) Now I had patience. 2) My genitals were squeaky clean.

After toweling off, I brushed my teeth and ran a comb through my hair. My hair used to require a brush back in my hippie days. Back then, long hair was synonymous with peace, love, and gifted musicians waiting for their genius to set them apart from the statis quo.

With my newfound patience, I opted to stretch out on the living room couch, instead of crawling up in the bed with her. There I could get some much-needed rest while keeping her backfield in motion, and the ball in my court.

Around about dusky dark, I was awakened by Esmeralda sliding the army issue footlocker across the living room floor on the entry rug. She'd managed to unload it from the top of her Volkswagen. She'd also managed to sweep most of the snow off before she brought it inside. After my eyes had drawed up to a focus, I could see the trunk was still encased in a heavy coating of crystal-clear ice. She slid it up near the hearth to thaw.

"Hey Babe!" I greeted her with a sleepy smile. (Terms of endearment are something I use with women I'm sexually attracted to… whether I know them or not!)

I'd been dreaming of Esmeralda… feeling her up in my sleep. Evidently, I was unable to cope with her hairy legs in my dream... so I covered them with ice cream. Go figure!

"Hey Lefty! She retorted. I didn't mean to wake you up." "No worries, I say. Did you rest well?" I ask in a caring tone. "Like a baby!" She replied holding her palms together laying her cheek against them in a show of slumber.

Esmeralda looked sexy in the red and black flannel shirt I'd loaned her. It was too broad in the shoulders, but it made the sleeves fit just about right on her long slender arms.

The sweatpants were tucked inside a pair of my cowboy boots she'd decided to appropriate on her own. The sharp pointed shit kickers looked like oversized clown shoes on her! I looked down at her feet and couldn't help but laugh.

"I hope you don't mind. I borrowed a pair of your boots to wade the snow in. Hope that's okay?" Esmeralda said apologetically. "Well... I guess so... just as long as you don't run off and join the circus on me!" I said sarcastically.

She shifted her head to one side and gave me a 'go to Hell look.' For the first time since we'd shared company, Esmeralda smiled at me with a big toothy grin. Her teeth were so bright they shone like a Pepsi dent commercial. It was easy to see she took great pride in them. Her gums were as pink as a Mary Kay Cosmetics car. Healthy strong teeth right down to her bicuspids. In the place of what most people call ... 'Eye Teeth,' Esmeralda had fangs!

She answered the question on my face before I could summon the right words to ask the question properly. "No... They're not real... No... I wasn't born with them no more than most call girls are born with vivacious tits. Truth is... my fangs are implants, just like the boobs of call girls are. What a prostitute and I have in common is simply this: "Implants make us both more marketable."

I settled back on the couch to digest all she'd just told me. After everything made perfect sense, I said: "I know what a call girl does for a living. I understand how Boobs would be an asset at the bargaining table for a prostitute. What I fail to see is how vampire teeth would help anyone... except for maybe... Oh let me see... a Vampire?"

Esmeralda laughed, then she flopped down beside me on the couch and pointed her knees in my direction with her hands pursed between them. After she'd made eye contact, she began to explain. "I'm a medium... I'm a 'go between' for people among the living, who wish to communicate with those among the dead. My teeth help me to... shall we say... look the part."

"That makes perfect sense," I said. I've heard of people like you on late night radio. I've always considered ghosts and goblins and shadow people... Big Foot and Rougarou's... parallel universes and UFO's... as fiction. Stories told like they were really true for their entertainment value."

"Big Foot is real! She blurts out as if she were offended. They love and hurt and feel just like humans! They have families and skills You'll never be so lucky as to acquire! They live in a parallel universe where greed and hate and jealousy are beneath them!

They inhabit a spectral plain where they can pass back and forth between a myriad of separate realities."

"I kind of get it I tell her... What I really want to tell her is this... "Sounds like a bunch of hocus pocus horse hockey to me!" Once again, the ball is in her court. Like in tennis, Server wins deuce point. The only reason I'm not already down for the count is because of the patience I gained in the shower. It's her serve... but all is fair in love and war, so I come out of left field with a curve ball...

"Do you know how to make snow ice cream?" Knowing my question had no relevance to our apparitional conversation, I was not at all surprised when she offered no reply. When I asked her, "Do you want another shot?" Her facial expression told me that ghosts were not the only Spirits she'd become intimately accustomed to.

CHAPTER
NINE

After we'd knocked back half a fifth of Jack Black, she slid her footlocker up next to the coffee table. It had completely defrosted setting over by the stove. Esmeralda opened the lid and peered inside, as if she were doing a mental inventory of the locker's contents.

"I have some things I'm excited to show you for the seance tonight." Esmeralda reached in with her long slender arms and pulled out something adorned in a Golden shimmering tapestry. "This is my Ouija Board," she said proudly as the tapestry slid away.

"This particular board has no manufacture's stamp, because it wasn't manufactured.

What it does have, is a "maker's mark." I've been told by several reliable sources that it was made in Louisiana swamp country by an alchemist and Witch Doctor named, Frater Albertus, back in the early 1800's. See the triangle with a Purple Amethyst in the center? That was his 'Makers Mark'.

Albertus' work was known far and wide for its quality. Albertus himself was known for the power in his magic. Here... hold it!" she insisted.

"This thing weighs a ton!" I say in amazement. "It's solid marble. She replied, then continued. All the letters and numerals are inlaid with Black Onyx." Her eyes grew even larger as she leaned over in front of me, pointing out the board's fine craftsmanship.

I watched spell bound as her eyes began to capture the deep dark tones of the Black Onyx. Her pupils began to reflect the powerful magic in her Ouija.

With eyes ablaze, she continued.

"Now this particular Ouija she proclaimed, was said to have been the property of none other than the infamous Josie Arlington. Ms. Arlington was Madam of an also infamous brothel in the New Orleans' Red light district, better known as... Storyville."

"Oh... I've heard of Storyville! Louie Armstrong cut his teeth playing trumpet in those houses of ill repute." I stand and try to return the Ouija back to Esmeralda, but she won't take it from me. "Wait just a minute... set back down," she insisted. I placed the Ouija Board back on my lap and leveled it on my knees.

She leaned over the footlocker and retrieved a small rather authentic looking alligator. After closer examination, I noticed it was in fact authentic. A rather nice piece of taxidermy. It had shiny scales and a dead tied look of dispossession in its cold clammy eyes.

From its mouth, Esmeralda extracted a heart shaped object with a hole hewn in the center. "This is the planchette," she explained. It slides around on the Ouija and answers questions the medium asks of it by spelling out words and landing on numbers. Here... let me show you."

She sat the planchette on the Ouija Board as I held it in my lap. She spread her long slender fingers and placed them lightly on the board. The planchette began to spin uncontrollably, then flung itself off the board angrily.

Esmeralda burst forth in a state of shock accompanied by a shrill uncanny fit of laughter. When she regained herself, the words she spoke unnerved me. "You're a Born again Christian, aren't you?"

"You're Damn right I am! Washed in the blood!" "Well, you must be died in the wool too she retorted, because my board doesn't like you for shit!" I stood up with the board outstretched in her direction.

"Here! You better take this damn thing before I throw it in the fire!" Esmeralda seemed to shrink back in the early evening shadows as she came to the realization that it was cold outside, and that she was fixin' to be put out on her ass, Ouija Board and all!

"Lefty, now Lefty just calm down. I didn't mean to upset you. I'm sorry I upset you lefty. How about I fix you a drink?... You want snow Ice cream? I can make snow ice cream if you want?... Do you have any vanilla ex-tract?" Esmeralda asked, while she wrapped the Ouija in its tapestry cloth and tucked it back in the footlocker.

I stood there pondering in silence wondering how in the hell I'd ended up snowed in with a fucking witch... in my own fucking house! I watched Esmeralda's countenance soften as she waited submissively for the answer to her question.

"There's Vanilla extract in the cabinet, but don't worry about that now. She smiled knowing that I too, had softened some. "How about that drink then?" She asked. "Yeah... you can fix me a drink... make it a double... Hell woman... bring two glasses and the whole damn bottle! We may as well get shit faced... It's not like we could go anywhere even if we wanted to!"

"Good idea!" She said over her shoulder baring her fangs like a vampire slut in a Bela Lugosi movie. I could tell by the look she flashed me, that the mystery and romance of being snowed in with a stranger that was not a perfect gentleman, had an allure all its own for her.

Esmeralda came back with two tumblers, a shot glass, and a brand new fifth of Jack Black. She greeted me with a kiss on her arrival. I'd tasted her lips earlier, when we decided that playing 'Spin the bottle' would be the perfect way to end the night... or begin the night... if kissing just so happened to take us past the point of no return. When she kissed me this time, I knew Esmeralda was mine for the taking. As for me, the patience I had gained earlier that day in the shower... was long gone!

Somewhere on her trip to the kitchen to fetch the booze, Esmeralda had managed to smooth on a silky coat of luscious Red lipstick. I tried not to smudge it, but when my tongue found hers, we kissed deeply. When my tongue found her vampire teeth it excited me so, that I felt Ole Porky rise past my belly button, and out the top of my Wranglers. Esmeralda felt it too!

Before I knew what was happening, both my hands were full of her thick Gypsy hair. Each time her slender throat struggled against my ravenous hunger, I dug my fingers deeper into her hair.

I lunged in ecstasy as the last surge of my hot lava scorched a trail to the depths of her willing throat. When I looked down at my Gypsy girl, her eyes were rolled back in her head, but the creamy smile on her face told me she was one happy witch!

Esmeralda threw her arms around my shoulders and hugged me, then she picked up the Jack Black, and turned the bottle up. She set the bottle down and fell back on the couch.... She was out like a light!

Feeling invigorated from the amazing oral copulation, I went to the window and looked out. The snowstorm was still raging. All that could be heard was the wind racing around the corners of the house, and the occasional pop from the wood stove.

I dug in the cabinet under the kitchen sink for a bottle

of Southern Comfort Sammy Katz brought me for a birthday gag gift the last time he'd come out to throw horseshoes.

That was back in August around my birthday. Everybody who knows me, knows I'm a Jack Black man. Still, I was glad to have the sticky sweet liquor.

I broke the seal and took a good pull. There was still half a fifth of Jack Black on the coffee table, but Esmeralda had turned up the bottle after I'd blowed my load, and I wasn't taking any chances on her backwash.

I reached for my breast pocket and pulled out a crush proof box of cowboy killers, but all the killers were gone. Being as I was a Boy Scout early in life, "Be Prepared," had become a motto for me early on. I went to the nightstand and pulled a fresh pack of Marlboro's from the top drawer.

About the time I lit up, I heard a loud crash followed by a fireworks display that lit up the backyard! Then everything went Black. A tree had fallen across the power lines.

With my trusty Zippo still in hand, I took the Brakeman's lantern from a shelf in the laundry room and lit it. I turned the knob that trims the wick until the smoke stopped, and the flame burned blue with just a little yellow flickering around the edges.

I hadn't used the lantern since I'd fished Smokey Hill River back last Spring. Coleman lanterns are brighter, but they have to be pumped up every so often. The glass globes break too easily, the asbestos mantels turn into ashes and fall apart with the slightest bump. Coleman lanterns make a hiss that just so happens to annoy the Hell out of me! "Light a coal oil lantern and forget about the fuss!" That's what I say.

The combination of Jack Black and Southern Comfort had evidently joined forces.

The two Spirits had obviously paired together before... just never in my gullet!

I set down in the living room rocking chair so that I could rock back and forth, instead of going round and round. After I was seated, I could hear the wind howl, the stove pop, and the rocking chair creek. Once those sounds settled in on me, I closed my eyes and drifted off to dream... or so I thought.

In my dream I heard a voice calling out to me: "Wefty... Wefty... hey

Wefty... you need to turn that dad gum ole Ouija Board off man! Hey Dude!!! The Gypsy Chick?... she never closed the dad gum board out man! I've been fighting those dad gum Spirits off all night! Wefty... hey Wefty... if you don't dad gum listen to me and turn that board off, you're gonna have every dad gum ghost from the train station in your living room!"

The thought of having a living room full of ghosts was enough to shake me out of a dream, even though I wasn't dreaming... The goofy sounding voice I was hearing just kept on talking. The voice was kind of crisp and had an obvious speech impediment.

There was a happy-go-lucky kind of joyful quality to it that couldn't be denied as well. Almost every statement was punctuated with a chuckle!

I picked up the railroad lantern and searched every corner in the living room. The further from the wood stove I got, the more I was convinced that the happy voice was coming from the stove and reverberating in the stovepipe. I double checked to make sure I wasn't in the middle of a crazy dream. I even slapped myself to make sure I was awake. Floating on the wind outside, I could hear what sounded like a choir of ghoulish laughter.

"Hey Wefty... Wefty... can you hear them dad gum poltergeisters? They gonna Bum Rush you Man if you don't close the portal on that Gypsy's Ouija Board Dude! Wefty... Hey Wefty... open the dad gum stove door Dude!"

"I ain't opening my damn stove door just because some happy assed, tongue tied, disembodied, paranormal, hocus-pocus, funky ass ghost with a cleft pallet and a speech impediment says so... "Ha! Ha! Okay Wefty... Have it your way!"

CHAPTER

TEN

No sooner had the disembodied voice rattled up the stovepipe, when all Hell broke loose! I heard doors in the back of the house open, then slam shut! Drawers and cabinet doors swung wildly. I could hear plates and dishes slamming against the wall!

I sat in the Livingroom rocker, clutching the railroad lantern as if it were my only hope for salvation. I was afraid to know what was going on in the back of the house. Finally, I summoned the courage to look over my shoulder. When I did, I saw the couch rise up off the floor halfway to the ceiling.

Esmeralda was still in a reclining position, but she was floating even higher than the couch! The coffee table spun clockwise on one leg, while the half full bottle of Jack Black danced like a runway model up one coffee table leg, then down the other!

"All right you fricking chuckle head I shouted, slinging open the stove door. How do I shut the Gypsy bitch's board down?... Chuckle Head!... Chuckle Head! C'mon Man! Tell me how to close the portal! Don't make me come in there after you motherfucker!"

I heard a chuckle so loud it made the stovepipe rattle, then the cast iron door slammed shut hard, and the damper closed. Everything floating in the air came crashing down except for Esmeralda. She was being passed around by a bunch of poltergeists, like she was in a mosh pit!

I was standing their gape mouthed in a state of disbelief when the cast iron door flew open. A rage of flame leaped forth like it had come from a dragon's mouth! I was expecting the worst that could happen when I heard a chuckle rattle in the stovepipe... then from the belly of the stove came one singular word that changed everything... STOP!!!

Esmeralda dropped like a rock. She had been floating higher than the only picture hanging on my living room wall! After that, the only sound that could be heard was Esmeralda cussing me out for allegedly throwing her off the couch. She took a few hard pulls from the bottle, then with another string of unintelligible cuss words, she passed back out.

"Geezzz Dude! You ready to dad gum listen to me now Wefty?" I hesitated with my reply. I was still in search of what was left of my sanity. Hearing a stove talk... much less calling out your name? ... That's freaking nuts! Validating Chuckle Head in the stove by responding to his question... That's bat shit crazy!

As I stood there in the process of making a solemn vow to myself never to mix Jack Black and Southern Comfort again, I heard Chucklehead's voice come out of the stove.

"Ha! Ha! Hey Wefty... Throw a chunk of coal in the dad gum ole stove, then you can see me." I weighed my options... I could rebut a stove... or I could throw a chunk of coal in it... I chose the ladder. When I did, the flame turned from reds and yellows... to a wavy transparent gas stove blue. Peering through the open stove door, I looked dead in the face at Chucklehead! "Ha! Ha! ... Hey Wefty!"

Riding on a clean blue flame was the image of a long-faced man with smoke white hair, and a beard that waved on the flame. His beard hung down into the belly of the stove beyond my line of vision. His wrinkled face would stretch smoothly on the crest of the flame, then topple back on the stove's convection currents and wrinkle again.

"Who the Hell are you? What the Hell are you?" "Ha! Ha! One dad gum thing at a time there Wefty. Go get that Ouija Board!" I was not used to taking orders from a ghost, but under the circumstances, I reassured myself that this was all just delirium trimmers caused from mixing Tennessee Whiskey with Southern Comfort.

Tomorrow this nightmare would be laughable, but tomorrow wasn't here yet.

I extracted the Ouija Board from Esmeralda's footlocker. When I did, the alligator came to life and latched on my shirt sleeve viciously! He began to roll violently until I slung him off my sleeve and stomped him with the heel of my cowboy boot.

When I did, the planchette came flying out of his mouth and set up a spin like it had earlier that evening.

I kicked the planchette with the toe of my sharp pointed shit kicker. "Take that you son of a bitch!" I shouted as it bounced off the wall. I grabbed it up and headed back to the rocking chair with the Ouija Board under my right arm, and the planchette clinched tightly in my left fist. "Ha! Ha!... Good job Wefty!

Now, Chucklehead instructed. Put the board on your knees and place the planchette over the maker's mark." I could feel the planchette resisting, but I did as Chuckle Head told me. When I did, the board glowed to incandescence. I could smell the Ouija's evil!

It exuded a rotten stench somewhere between burning flesh, and putrid swamp water. The board's glow chilled my bones as it singed off most of my fingerprints. Just when I thought I could hold it no longer, the planchette quivered violently, but I held it to the Maker's Mark until the gray marble board encrusted with Black Onyx dimmed to darkness... and faded behind the yellow light of the Brakeman's lantern.

The sun was on the horizon when Jazzy woke me whining, and running in circles.

She needed to pee... Sad to say it was a little too late for me... I'd done gone and pissed the bed!

Esmeralda lay face down with my cowboy boots dangling off the edge of the couch. That girl was a long one she was!

Unbeknownst to me, but according to last night's conversation, Chucklehead's Spirit had been living in the stove a long time before the old Kansas City Southern depot was unfunded and eventually disassembled.

Ole Chucklehead started out as a Pullman Porter during the Civil War. Most of the passengers he tended back then were commissioned officers. Chucklehead was a little off center, but he had already lived a long time before he died, so I guess he had the right.

His name was Charles Cullen. Chuck was of Irish decent even though he was raised in Georgia on Lookout Mountain. A tiny little town called Rising Fawn.

As best as I recall, his father had been a migrant worker who found employment at a Plantation sawmill when he'd come to America from Ireland. Chuck was born on the Plantation in a slave cabin.

Like his father before him, Chuck worked the sawmill coming up. I can't recall just how Chuck came to work for the railroad, but he did, right up to his death.

He catered to top military Brass as a Porter during the

height of the Civil War. Chuck mentioned serving Ulysses S. Grant and smoking Cuban cigars with him.

William Tecumseh Sherman always tipped generously. Chuck mentioned other famous generals that I may be able to recall after I recover from this God-awful hangover!

After the war, Chucklehead became a Water Tender for Kansas City Southern. He lived at the depot servicing trains when they needed to take on boiler water, and kept the train station warm in the wintertime.

At the request of the Union Army, and Ulysses S. Grant himself, Chucklehead was once again appointed as General Grant's personal porter on his campaign trail while he made his bid for the White House.

Chucklehead got quiet after that. I tried to get him to tell me more, but he wouldn't say much, only that he had been shamed by General Grant, and cursed by a witch named Ballam.

Chuck said he died in a boiler explosion, and that it served him right! Coal is to Chuck, what whisky is to me... He said he don't talk much without a good chunk of coal to bolster him. We talked most all night, or at least until the coal ran out… that's when Chucklehead got the blues.

It could have all just been a dream... but it sure felt real to me! After drinking Jack Black all evening, then mixing it with Southern Comfort, anything is possible! There is only one way to know for sure.

Chuck told me that if I pulled the moss away from that drippy leg on the third water tank, I would find a secret door in the leg's concrete foundation. If there is a secret door, then I'll know that there is another world I was never aware of. A world just beyond the veil of this reality.

CHAPTER

ELEVEN

Jazzy pawed at me until I woke that afternoon a couple of hours before dark. When I went to make coffee, I found the carafe broken into a million pieces. Plates and dishes, coffee cups and saucers, lay strewn everywhere. One cabinet door was off its hinges from last night's unruly chain of events. I went to the living room to check on Esmeralda. She was long gone. Ouija Board, footlocker, Volkswagen and all.

Even though the daylight hours were mostly gone, it was plain to see that the Arctic blast had been ushered out on a southern breeze. The sun looked like a polished lemon hanging at the edge of a powder blue sky. Before the early Autumn blast, the nighttime temperatures had not fallen much below the sixty-degree mark, so the soil was still warm.

The calf deep snow that had accumulated so rapidly

yesterday, was now beating a hasty retreat in turbulent little streams running beneath what was left of the icy slush. Ole Blue still had snow in the truck bed, but the cab and the windshield had melted off completely.

Traipsing on a translucent layer of slush, I made my way to Ole Blue's driver door. I lifted the leaver and tipped the old-fashioned bench seat forward. Tucked in up underneath the coil springs where the cops are less likely to find it, is my backup stash of Jack Black.

Now any respectable drunk, who is a drunk in good standing. Any drunk that has not fooled around and lost his drinking privileges. Why Hell... even a "has-been drunk," or a "wanna-be-drunk," knows the one saying that is synonymous with all drunks everywhere after a good bender...

"What a feller needs... is a little bit-o-the hair from the tail of the dog that bit him."

Being a true believer in this ancient mantra, I twist off the lid and get myself a good pull from my stash bottle. Then I get one more just for the burn. (A good snoot full always helps to fend off the inevitable hangover.) A few more pulls made me feel some better. After I did, I walked around back looking for storm damage. There wasn't much to see other than the Red Oak, and the power line that it had fallen on.

When I got back to the house, I called the R.E.C. and reported my power outage. Then I picked up the broken dishes. As I did, I found the only coffee cup that still had a handle. Then I loaded the trash can with the big pieces of broken glass, and swept up the slivers from all the plates, glasses and cups that didn't make it through last night's ghost riot. All that went unscathed was the flatware.

Everywhere I looked there is undeniable proof that last night was more than just a bad mix of booze and delirium tremors.

It Seems I've always learned about life and love the hard way. Who knows... maybe there is a "Big Foot!" All I know for sure is... I wanna' be asleep when this hangover hits me!

I woke up around my usual time that next morning with 12 hours of passed out sleep under my belt. The roosters had just begun to crow, but the sun was still yet to shine across the freshly shorn prairie.

Jazzy was off to the backdoor dancing her usual morning pee dance. For the first time in days, I had wakened in my own bed. I'd slept in the jail house for two nights, rode a combine all night the third night, and slept in my rocking chair on the fourth night... talking to a ghost!

I'd pretty much managed to circumvent the hangover that always comes when I'm foolish enough to drink anything but Jack Black or Cold Beer. All and all, I'd slept through the worst of it. Considering the hell I'd been through, I felt pretty good. I did however sport a hangover headache. You know... the kind of headache where you feel like your brain has come loose, and is subject to bounce around in your skull if you move too fast? I figure the hangover was aggravated by the unique combination of starvation... and dehydration.

I cupped my hands around the kitchen sink faucet and sucked like a camel filling its hump. When I'd had my fill, I headed for the hen house. Bacon and eggs, hash browns and buttered toast. That's what's for breakfast!

I gathered six brown eggs in my cowboy hat and let the gals out to free range. Once the nests were empty, I discovered a rat snake curled up in a corner box. He was just finishing up his breakfast when our eyes met.

As a younger man, I'd kill any snake I came across. Once a man gets enough age on him that he realizes he too is stamped with an expiration date, live and let live becomes a much more acceptable mantra to live by.

I took the sawed-off cane pole from the corner that I keep handy for such occasions and dislodged him with it. He and I have been through this routine a hundred times before. He always gets that, "Don't Taze me Dude!... Don't Taze me!" look in his eyes... then slithers off with a quickness.

I stopped by the lawnmower shed to fetch my trusty ole campfire coffee pot since those damn poltergeists broke my Mr. Coffee. It's dented up some, but it's seasoned in good, so it makes a super surly cup-o-Joe.

There on a shelf behind where the brakeman's lantern usually sets, I find a dusty Mason jar full of Blackberry jelly, Kory Katz had preserved a couple of summers back.

I remember that day well... how proud she was of it... and how good it tasted on her freshly baked biscuits at breakfast that next morning. I almost asked her to marry me that day. I never could bring myself to it. She was only 40... and much too young and full of life to be this old man's widow.

I stood lost in her memory for a moment, wondering how my life would be now had I asked her? Maybe it's only wishful thinking, but I'm purdy sure she would have said "Yes!"

Being as my headache had given way to the ache in my heart, and that my belly was beginning to think my throat had been cut. I placed the jar of jelly in the coffee pot, the screwdriver in the shed's hasp, and stepped it on back to the house with coffee pot in one hand, and my hat full of eggs in the other.

I had planned on fried rabbit for the Fall season's first meal cooked on the woodstove, but I learned long ago, that life is what happens while we're busy making plans. I think John Lennon said that. Some say he stole it from Allan Saunders. Who ever said it first don't matter much. It was as true for one as it was 'tuther... and true for me as either of them.

Once we finished eating breakfast, I thrust ole Jazzy girl up on the bed. Her belly was full too! Rarely do we eat without one another. She circles with excitement in anticipation of me stretching out on the bed so she can nestle her muzzle up under my arm pit. At her age and mine, napping has become one of those simple pleasures we have come to enjoy in our latter years.

I awoke mid-afternoon as the chill of an early Fall reminds me that even though Old Man Winter was not fully upon us yet, he had slipped his calling card under the threshold. Every window in the old house leaks hot air in Summer, and cold air in Winter.

I was still trying to come to terms with Chuckle Head, and all the paranormal b.s. that Esmeralda introduced me to. For the time being, it was easier to stay drunk than it was to face the truth.

I'd sift through ashes in the wood stove until the glow of embers would appear. I'd add kenneling and stove wood but not coal. I wasn't ready to see Chucklehead again. The last thing I needed was my foundation to be shaken further.

All the events from that night had tangled up my mind to a point that I was in denial. Knowing myself as I do, it would take a good long talk with the man in the mirror for me to even begin sorting out my thoughts from all that had transpired. Meanwhile, I was not ready to come to terms with any of it yet! My only intention back then was to breathe in... and breathe out!

Halloween was still a few weeks away, but the pumpkin patch was ready to be harvested. The soon to be 'Jack-O-Lanterns,' were Orange as hot weather moons. The vines that had been a blushing Green only days before, had turned brown and shriveled like a severed umbilical cord.

When the ground was dry enough to get Ole Blue out to the truck patch, Jazzy supervised as I rounded up a heaping load of pumpkins that were big as a hog's head! Ole Blue was down on his overloads when we drove them over to Tote-A-Poke and sold them all for one money. I could have made more at a roadside stand, but Mr. Lawson, the produce manager, always treats me fair on everything that comes from the truck patch. He wrote me a check for might near $300.00.

After the early Arctic blast had come in like a lion, it rode off into the sunset like yesterday's cowboy. Indian Summer had wrapped her graceful arms around my little Central Kansas home again. The agreeable weather was spent tilling a years' worth of chicken poop into the soil. Along with a years' worth of grass clippings, potato peelings, coffee grounds, and whatever else ended up in the compost pile.

The next few days were spent insulating waterpipes and hanging plywood on the chicken house to block out the winter wind. The "Farmer's Almanac." was predicting a "Particularly cold winter." This they said was due to the jet stream, or the alignment of Jupiter and Mars… or some other such sort of astrological hocus pocus.

Once I had all my own ducks in a row, I loaded up the "Gravely" self-propelled front tine tiller, and headed toward town to Doctor Fred Phillips house. Each year, I turn over the soil in their vegetable garden, as well as Connie's flower beds. I do this once in the Spring, and once again in the Fall. Unbeknownst to Connie… Doc pays me with a fifth of Jack Black… Connie thinks I do it so my visits to the Chiropractic Office never reach the billing department. Unbeknownst to Doc, I graciously except the cash tip Connie never fails to give me.

Being as I was already in town, I went by the Courthouse Annex and picked up a check for "Lost Wages" that Judge Harris had granted me for what he deemed as… inappropriate incarceration. The lost wages check was equal to the "final harvest check" Mr. Kramer paid me in actual wages for final harvest. Counting the money for the sale of pumpkins, plus the forty bucks Connie tipped me for tilling, I was setting on Twelve Hundred and Forty Dollars! Enough to pay my mortgage for a year, with 40 bucks to spare!

I set on a park bench outside the Courthouse Annex feeling purdy satisfied with myself. I watched a crew of city employees hang Halloween decorations for about an hour. Soon, some of my own pumpkins from the truck patch would be carved and displayed along with a vast variety of witches and ghosts and goblins and all manner of ghoulish gaiety. Halloween was always a festive competition between merchants on Town Square. The outlandish extravaganza, was only to be bested by the lavish Yuletide decorations at Christmas.!

On the way back home, Jazz and I stopped in at

Poskey's, "Gas For Less." We stopped in to fill up and check the mail. The toe headed pit crew greeted us with their usual vigor. "Fill'er up Lefty?" Says one. "Check under the hood Sir?" asks another. The child relegated to making sure that every tire is checked for proper air pressure? He bobs his head up and gives me an almost military report... "All good Sir!"

The eldest child that always polishes my windshield till it shines? She is no longer a child with budding breasts, she's turned into a full-fledged woman! "Here's your mail Sir," says the youngest of Mr. Poskey's pit crew. As always happens, the young lady brings Jazzy a treat. Once again, we're on our way, but only after a smile and a hometown wave from the proprietor, Mr. Jack Poskey.

News on the truck radio spiels the usual chatter of things that by enlarge, don't affect me much. I've never invested in the stock market, or the commodities market. Commodities to me are salt and pepper, flower and sugar and cornmeal. A tub of lard, and of course... a 20-pound bag of Pinto beans just in case times get hard.

By and by, the weatherman gets his turn at the microphone. His tone of voice tells me he's holding back, like the big bad wolf did with Red Riding Hood? He's totally enthralled with the prospect of being 'The Weather God'... again!

It was almost palpable to me when he expounded on the upper-level trade wind pattern shift. How unstable air masses can erupt with a vengeance at the drop of a hat. We need a weatherman who is for us… not against us. Somebody needs to fire that son of a bitch before he freezes us all to death!

I haven't built a fire for more than two weeks, with the exception of a few sticks of kenneling to knock off the chill at morning. Not a roaring fire…no… that might awaken the ghost in my stove. Just a small fire to knock off the chill has done nicely.

The last real fire I had, was when Esmeralda and her creepy assed Ouija Board filled my head with the undeniable truth that a parallel universe does exist, just beyond this world's timeline continuum.

Until I'm ready to come to grips with the fact that there's a ghost living in my wood stove, I'd rather not think about the ghostly ghastly occurrences that happened only a fortnight hence. Though I try to put it out of my mind during my waking hours, few nights are those when it doesn't dominate my dreams in slumber.

When November comes, the old wood stove will begin its seasonal roar. My only choice at that point will be to find reconciliation in the restoration of my old truths, and except my newfound truths along with them. Hopefully, they will homogenize, and give me a broader perspective as I come to better understand the nature of things.

CHAPTER

TWELVE

At dawn next morning while sipping coffee, I decided it's about time to get up a goodly supply of stove wood for the Winter that will soon be staring me in the face.

The Rural Electric Cooperative, had cut just enough limbs from the large Red Oak to retrieve their power line that came down with it in the storm. With the six ricks of stove wood, I've already cut and stacked, the addition of the downed Red Oak should do nicely until Spring breathes her honeysuckle breath across the land once again.

While setting on the porch sharpening my chainsaw, I noticed that the windmill's blades lumbered along at a usual pace, but the fan was facing a southwestern direction. Rather an oddity for this time of year.

I remember hearing something conspiratorial in the

weatherman's voice this morning on the radio. I could tell the egotistical bastard had something up his sleeve. Something in his countenance raised my hackles and made me uneasy, but that thought wouldn't occupy my head for long, I had wood to cut.

The chain saw bit deep into the course beautiful Auburn grain of the downed Red Oak. A flurry of long slender shavings pelted my mid drift as I set the dawgs deep and pulled up hard on the handle. That makes the old 'Farm Boss 41 bite like a junkyard dog!

The old STIHL has long since lost his luster, but he's still all man! He may be old, but he shines when it comes down to gut and muscle!

"Field & Stream" magazine notably stated in an article pertaining to the logging industry, that those who fell timber for a living agreed to the man, that the Farm Boss 41 was… "One of the best chainsaws 'STIHL' ever made!"

I found the ole '41,' stuffed in a corner of the lawnmower shed preserved in a five-gallon bucket of hydraulic oil. He had neither bar nor chain. It took a "Parts Bath" to wash all the oil out of that old, "Living Legend!" Turn the switch to the (ON) position: Pull out the (CHOKE)… And by God, be ready to cut some wood!

After the saw work was done, I chunked the bed of Ole Blue three times full and rounded up… till he squatted on his axles! Then, with Jazzy supervising, I stacked each load neatly on the back porch under the roof and against the weather. Needless to say, by that time my back was killing me!

Killing two birds with one stone may not be all it's cracked up to be, but the fact is... I needed to walk so I don't get stove up. I needed to walk because I'm tired of running from the fact that there really is a ghost living in my stove!

I've replaced all my dishes and my Mr. Coffee. Now it's time for me to admit to myself that the reason I had to, was because the poltergeist broke my old ones, "Frickin' Assholes!"

I set out across the yard to walk the railroad tracks. Just before I straddled the barbed wire fence, I remembered the small toy coal bucket someone left behind the stove when I was in jail.

I thought about how hunched over I was, and how hard it is to pick up my feet when I'm down in the back.

Even though I dreaded the front porch steps, I went back and fetched the coal bucket anyway. "May as well pick up a few chunks of coal for ole Chucklehead, he likes his coal like I like my whiskey, and we need to talk a few things out." I say to myself.

Unless it was delirium trimmers brought on from mixing Jack Daniels and Southern Comfort... (and I know it wern't.) Ole Chuckle Head said coal does for him... what Jack Black does for me... mellows him out some, soze he can visit more comfortable like.

When I hung the coal bucket on a "T" post to cross the

fence, I saw a smudged piece of notebook paper folded up lying on the bottom. I dusted the coal suet off and folded it one more time, then stuffed it in my britches pocket.

After I'd lumped my bad leg over the fence, the pants leg of my good leg snagged on the barbed wire and sent me sprawling headfirst into the tall Johnson grass. I lay there for a minute laughing at myself and wondering how I'd ever come to be this way.

I thought back to my teenage years, and those track meets in high school. Back when hurdles taller than the barb wire fence I'd just tripped over, was cleared with ease. How catching your toe on a hurdle would leave you fighting for that superb degree of balance that can never be regained… once you've lost it.

In my sprawl, I scared up a covey of quail that departed with a noisy clatter of flapping wings. In my youth, the occasion would have afforded me at least two birds down with Daddy's double-barreled shotgun, if ole Lil and Eddie were on the hunt with me. By God there ain't nothing in this world better than a good dog!

Jazz wouldn't make a pimple on a bird dog's ass... but she sure can draw a crowd when she points her muzzle up toward Heaven and breaks out with a mournful howl while I'm playing on a street corner… "She's licking my face now."

Everything that had been late summer green, has lost its vibrant color, and faded away to death nail brown, except for the railroad ties. They are a mixture of moss green patina, and sun-bleached gray.

The only train I've ever seen on these tracks, was the train that hauled the old Depot away. After all the years of abandonment, chunks of coal can still be found. The exposure to sunlight and weather doesn't seem to affect coal much, being a fossil fuel and all.

I use railroad spikes when I set limb lines on Smokey Hill River. They're heavy enough to carry the line as far as you can throw it, yet light enough to tell when there's a fish on the line. A feller what didn't know, might think they were made for that very purpose.

I walked far enough down the railroad tracks to come to an understanding with myself about Chucklehead... and Big Foot... and things that exist outside of my own ability to comprehend… or reason out.

I also came to the firm conclusion that cowboy boots and railroad ties are a bad combination! Railroad ties are spaced further apart than even a tall man's stride can stretch from one step to the next. Holding my arms out and trying to do a tight rope act on a railroad track used to be achievable to some degree when I was a kid... Now... it's just downright embarrassing!

Curiosity was getting the better of me as to what the note in my pocket might contain, so I stepped away from the tracks to find a place to set where I could read the notebook paper, I'd found in the coal bucket. I set out for a pile of flat rocks that were most likely to be a property line marker in times gone bye.

Just before I sat down, Jazzy caught my attention with a guttural growl. Then I heard it! The source of her contention. A sound that has no language barrier... a sound like the cocking of a gun... Tiny beads and a button!

Before I knew what happened, Jazzy was slinging a five-foot rattler in circles and popping its head like a buggy whip!

Her hair stood on end, and her eyes blazed with fury as she tangled in a life-or-death struggle with a Western Diamond Back Rattler! Jazz would circle one way and then the other, slinging the vipers' head against the rocks as it struck at its own body trying to sink its fiendish long curved fangs into its assailant. It curled and rolled and tumbled until it was overcome by what I suspect may have been its own venom!

I carried Jazzy all the way home under my arm. Periodically, I would set the coal bucket down to pet her and make a fuss over her. She had likely saved my life! With all the endorphins that had surged through my blood stream while my little Black and White Papillon was valiantly protecting me, my back straightened and the vertebrae in my back must have found their natural place... I was no longer hurting!

With a joyful sense of relief, I decided that it might be kind of nice having company on the cold Winter nights that lay ahead... even if it was a ghost with a rather profound speech impediment!

Jazzy had achieved hero status, and she knew it! My spine was back in alignment... and all was right with the world again. The walk had done us both a world of good!

After knocking the poison off a fresh fifth of Jack Black, I pulled the notebook paper from my britches pocket and began to read... The note was from Kory Katz!

Dear Lefty,

I heard you were in jail for beating Ben Hoover up!

Rumor has it that you shot him too! I hope that you're not in trouble bad? By the time I made it to the courthouse, they said you were already gone. I looked everywhere, but couldn't find you anywhere! I built a fire in your stove and waited up all night for you to come home. I set on the couch and cried, thinking about how much I love you, and how we should be together... but you think I'm too young for you... Lefty, my heart aches for you. My body yearns for you! No one could ever take your place! there will never, ever be anyone for me, but you Lefty!

Forever yours,

Kory.

Kory's signature lipstick kiss was embossed on the inside fold of the letter. I folded it back carefully, so as not to smudge her kiss. I put it in the cigar box I keep at the back of my sock drawer that contains dozens of other love letters I'd found in the oddest places.

When Kory and I were a couple, seldom were the

times I went to town without her mark on my cheek. Her lipstick was a color somewhere between Hot Pink and Candy Apple Red. It was a color that perfectly represented her delightful sensuality.

"So… it had been Kory who had built the fire while I was getting in the season's last harvest?" I bounced the heal of my palm off my forehead! "Daaa...I should have known it all along!"

In contemplation, I sat on the porch petting Jazz and watched the evening sky as clouds danced like spirit filled buffalo on a chilly northern breeze. I could see them marauding across the open prairie. They never seemed to stop. I watched until the restless sky grew somber and dark on the horizon, then finally faded to Black.

CHAPTER

THIRTEEN

By morning, it was plain to see that the blissful days of Indian Summer had migrated south. I didn't need a calendar to know that November had arrived.

I let Jazz out, stoked the fire, and put on a pot of coffee. While it perked, I pulled a gallon Ziplock bag from the freezer containing the resident rabbit that had been Jazzy's first and only kill. That is, until yesterday's rattle snake. I set the rabbit in a bowl of salted water to thaw in the fridge.

Fried rabbit, along with a skillet full of corn fritters, and a fresh pot of pinto beans. It would be this evening's dinner. I would cook everything on the wood stove. The first full evening meal cooked on the wood stove is kind of an annual celebration. A commemoration to pay homage to yet another Holiday Season that would be spent alone with the exception of my singing dog, and maybe a ghost this year.

Soon would come Thanksgiving... Then the cold of Winter would usher in Christmas, along with flannel shirts and eggnog. Nights spent in my rocking chair sipping whiskey, and dreaming dreams of days long past. If only I were a younger man, it would be easier for me to justify my longing for love... for touch...for Kory.

This will be my third Christmas without a tree. The third Christmas without mistletoe, or stockings, or garland, or a wreath hanging on the front door. Without Kory, Christmas has been reduced to merely setting alone with my singing dog.

Ignorance is bliss, or so I've heard it said. A child who has never put his tongue to an Ice cream cone in the dog days of Summer can't possibly miss what they've never had.

After coming off the road and settling down in Jeter, Kory would soon become my favorite flavor. Her love would become my addiction.

It all began on the fifth day of December, some three years past. Kory showed up with the Grand Cherokee loaded to the hilt with all she owned. Her rent was four days past due. County Line Liquor didn't hand out paychecks until that Friday, which happened to land on the fourth day of that December. The landlord gladly took her $435.00 which was her monthly rent. After her money was safely in his pocket, he demanded an exorbitant late fee that he knew she couldn't pay… $165.00.

"All debts are not public," he said. Some debts are private, He told her, why don't you come on in Miss Katz, you can pay me in private." Kory had become much more than a lover to me, she was also my best friend! The next day I drove Ole Blue over to Smokey Hill Pawn. A 'lack luster' establishment that resided on the far side of Smoky Hill.

Her landlord's seedy pawnshop was located strategically across the tracks in the commercial district where Government housing projects were numerous among the general theme of shanties and downtrodden squalor.

Previous to my arrival at the Pawn Shop, I stopped by the Arcade and fed Quarters into a crane machine until its jaws landed on a Gold encrusted Cracker Jack ring. After fishing it out, I held the ring up for examination… "This will do just fine!"

I parked Ole Blue beneath the pawn shop sign that read. "Prices were born here, and raised down the street."

A bell tinkled as I pushed my way through a heavy bar-clad door… "What can I do you for today," greeted a short stub of a man, dangling the short stub of a burned-out cigar.

"Are you Mr. Renaldo, I enquired? "You're in luck he said smugly… before he noticed the fire in my eyes.

"I have an 18 Karat Gold ring I'd like to pawn," I said

in a self-assured tone. He reached up and scratched the whisker stubble on his double chin, then glanced down the counter at a woman Kory had described to me as his wife. She was going through a coin collection.

"Well... let's see what you got," Said the dumpy little lardass as he tried to put on his poker face, but was not succeeding. I handed him the Cracker Jack ring and took up the conversation.

"Yeah… well, you see Sir, I was going to give this ring to my girlfriend for Christmas and ask her to marry me. Trouble is, she's late on rent, and her landlord, (the unscrupulous bastard,)... took her rent money, then wanted $165.00 more for late fees! She told him she didn't have it! "You want to know what that son of a bitch told her? He said he'd be glad to take it out in trade!"

I tried my best to get it out of her... but she wouldn't tell me his name. That's because she knows I'd cut him everywhere but the bottoms of his feet! ... I apologize for being so angry Mr. Renaldo, but any man... who is a man... would feel the same way! Wouldn't you?"

Lardass did not reply, he just looked down the counter with a telltale look on his guilty face. Good news is... she did tell me about you, Mr. Renaldo... She said you was a nice man, and you... or your wife, would probably loan me some cash against this ring."

About that time the woman down the counter raised her voice in a tone of excitement. "Honey, the chart says this Silver dollar is worth $145.50... That's more than we paid for the whole collection," She stated triumphantly. "Good for you...sell it Sweetheart," he told her in a monotonus voice.

I watched as the blood flushed out of his face toward his lower extremities. Picking the conversation right back up I said.

"Now you and I both know Mr. Renaldo, being this ring is 18 Karat Gold, it's worth twice the six hundred dollars I need to help my girlfriend out."

The blood ran back to his face with a vengeance as he realized he was being blackmailed. I could see that he was boiling, as he walked stiffly to the cash register and lifted the coin tray. He pulled six crisp One Hundred Dollar Bills from beneath it and cuffed the money in his chubby little hand.

As he walked back to the counter, he glowered at me with eyes like Satan's own. Leaning in forward, Lardass put his palms on the glass countertop, then leaned in even closer. He glanced first at his wife, who was still in her own little world with the coin collection. He leaned in even further. Under his breath he growled in a harsh whisper... "I'll get you for this you son of a bitch!"

I plucked the bills from his greedy little hand and slipped them in my pocket. As I did, he made a circle behind the counter and patted the bulge in his left front pants pocket, indicating to me that he was packing. Then he crossed his arms and leaned back. His voice boomed as he took on a tone of authority.

"Sorry Fella... I don't loan money on costume jewelry! Whoever sold you that ring, got over on you big time!"

I stepped away from the counter and slipped the arcade ring in my pants pocket on top of the hundred-dollar bills. "Thanks for your appraisal, Mr. Renaldo" I said, holding my head down with the superficial sound of disappointment in my voice. "That ring sure did look real to me!"

I walked across the floor and pulled open the door. Then I spun on my boot heel and looked him square in the face. I caught his glare, and shot back one of my own...

"Well Mr. Renaldo... win some... lose some!"

I stopped on my way back through Smokey Hill at "Mother Clucker's Poultry Palace," and picked up a big box of fried chicken for Kory.

Some women like their men to bring them chocolate, some like flowers… Kory always liked it when I brought her chicken. "Man did that girl love her some chicken!"

The memory came back all over me. A single tear rolled down my face in recollection. I called out her name in desperation, breaking my own spell.

Even with the spell broken, her memory continued to overtake me... her greasy lips that kissed me all over when I gave her back her rent money, plus the late fee the landlord wanted her to pay up in ass.

I think she may have still had chicken in her mouth

when she dropped to her knees and unfastened my belt buckle.

Loving her was easy, as trying to forget her was hard!

When I finally snapped out of it, I put on my Army issue camo coat, and went out back to feed the chickens.

I put an extra amount of straw in their nesting boxes. The weatherman's forecast called for a light dusting of snow that evening. I carried some wood in from the back porch and stacked it along the living room wall.

After dinner I brought the stove up from a low cooking fire in preparation for a warm morning. I banked the stove up with heavy round wood and closed down the damper to choke off the oxygen so the wood would not blaze up, but would char through the night.

Then I would have that long overdue talk with the man in the mirror. There would be no whiskey shots for me until I'd come to the cold hard truth of what would soon become my new reality.

The house was filled that evening with smells passed down over the centuries. Beans seasoned with smoked ham hocks rolling and tumbling in a deep cast iron pot. Corn fritters made with the simplest ingredients. Potatoes frying on the woodstove in hog lard with chunks of yellow onions sweetening the air with a nose tingling, mouthwatering aroma. Free range rabbit dipped in egg wash, then rolled in a mixture of flour seasoned with salt and pepper. Smells so delightful they fill a man's olfactory with most everything he needs in life, except for a woman's touch.

As for Jazzy, she is dancing in celebration as if she knows the main course is Mr. Cottontail! As for me, I'll slather Kory's blackberry jelly on my corn fritters. I'll revel in the knowing that it is better to have known love and lost, than to have never known love at all.

Maybe it's how we held hands and took turns saying the Blessing? Maybe it was her cooking? All I know is this: No meal I'll ever eat again will taste as good or have that special nourishment as when Kory and I broke bread together.

I let Jazz out to do her duty before bedtime. At dinner, she had eaten out of one of the new plates from our newly stocked cabinet. I split Mr. Cottontail down the center and gave her the bigger half, the lion's share.

After doing her duty, she waddled through the back door with a full belly headed for the bedroom. She was ready to hit the hay.

As for me, I was ready for a shot of Jack Black. I overcame the urge to indulge.

Knowing me as I do, I knew that one, would lead to two. I know myself well enough to know that two, would lead to the third. After three, talking to the man in the mirror might never come.

FOURTEEN

Morning came with a new mindset. The man in the mirror is as stubborn as myself.

I suppose his stance on the matters at hand should have been almost predictable, knowing he is actually, me.

With clear eyes he staired back into my own with the resolve of sober judgment. "Pull back the moss on the drippy leg of the third water tank, he said. If you find a secret door, then I'll consider taking Chucklehead a little more seriously.

I believe in God... I will not waver in my beliefs without proof positive that you're not just a damned fool who mixed Jack Daniels with Southern Comfort! Find the secret door... or bother me no more!"

The light dusting of snow the weatherman predicted had not come to fruition, but the ground was covered with frost and frozen hard as a cow's horn that next morning. Blades on the windmill spun up to a blur, then lulled back down to be counted.

I swung the brakeman's lantern back to the lawnmower shed and set it back on the shelf beside the fishing poles. Then in the far corner where the garden tools are kept, I chose a hoe and a square point shovel to scrape away the moss from beneath the drippy leg.

There on the far north leg of the third water tank was a patch of frozen moss, just as Chucklehead said there would be. The moss grew to the concrete foundation's edge, then dropped off into a scuttle, where soil erosion had occurred from the steady drip of yesteryears drippage. I started out with the square point shovel trying to scrape off the moss. Nothing doing... it was frozen hard as a rock!

Knowing that the noonday sun would thaw the ground and loose the mosses' stealthy grip, I opted to drink another cup of coffee and make a grocery list. From a kitchen cabinet drawer relegated for cookbooks and such as the like, I pulled a yellow legal tablet filled with Kory's beautiful cursive hand. In clean straight rows were page after page of grocery items Kory called: "Her Master List."

I opened the pantry door and took a mental inventory of the canned goods that needed to be replaced. Sugar was running low, as was lard and cornmeal... things I used often.

On a lower shelf covered by a tangle of cobwebs in

the pantry, was an assortment of canned pie fillings with which Kory made the most delightful pies and cobblers. Sometimes she would bake just to make the house smell good.

Now I look back on those days when we started every day under this ole roof together. I feel like such a fool for not just letting her have her way. All Kory really ever wanted to do, was love me.

Time had become my teacher. In retrospect, I've come to know the true meaning of these words: "Blindest are those who refuse to see!"

I tossed a gallon jug of milk from the fridge and a jar of mayonnaise that was probably alright, but just looked funky. I was down to half a stick of butter. I completed my list and headed out for Jeter Market. By the time I returned home from shopping, the thermometer on the front porch post read 38 degrees. It was time to scrape away the moss and find the secret door in the water tank leg… if there actually was one.

I started scraping away the moss from the tanks concrete slab.

The job was harder than I'd ever imagined it would be. The curly tendrils of the mosses' root system clung tightly to the course concrete.

Soon I'd shucked my camo coat, but was still sweating under my long johns. The day had warmed considerably by the time I'd scraped the moss to the tank's massive concrete footing. The slab showed no signs of a trap door, so I took the garden hoe and began to scrape the vertical edge of the foundation.

Soon a grid of stubbles began to show a regular pattern. Closer examination revealed the stubble to be steel bars placed at intervals to reinforce the concrete in its construction.

By that time, I'd shed another layer of clothes. I stepped off the slabs edge and looked in disgust at a massive pile of moss I'd managed to pile high in my fruitless efforts. I'd lost my patience with the whole damn project… screw this… I'm gonna' take a break and drink myself a beer!

Once inside, I popped a beer and put the canned goods on their designated shelves in the pantry. Normally, that would have been my first order of business on my return from shopping. "A place for everything… and everything in its place. Kory taught me that.

I sat at the kitchen table and finished my beer, then I opened another one. As I did, it occurred to me that I was missing something, something that my eyes had seen, but my mind had not. Maybe the secret door had eluded me because it was hidden in plain sight. Maybe I was looking too hard?

I grabbed another cold one from the fridge and waited to pop the top until I was setting on the ground and looking at the vertical foundation edge. I sipped along for a while studying it out hard. Just as my gut instinct had told me, the truth was hidden right there in plain sight!

There it was… plain as the nose on your face! The rebar's regularly spaced pattern showed a discrepancy. An area of about two feet by three feet had no rebar stubble!

Reinvigorated, I picked up the hoe and attacked the spot with vengeance. The hoe made no scraping sound like before. The hoe went deep, breaking loose both rich black soil and the moss that held it in place. Recessed about six inches in the concrete, came the unmistakable sound of metal against metal. The sound was muffled at first but rang true lick after lick as the hoe dislodged the remaining dirt around the secret door's threshold.

Soon I was staring at the cold hard truth… There was a door, a secret door that had been hidden away through decades of obscurity.

When I brushed it with my fingertips, I could tell it had been constructed with tightly spaced rivets like the boiler of a steam engine. The hinges were finely crafted and were attached by rivets as well. A heavy hasp opposite the hinges had been secured with a lock that would be in itself, a challenge to remove.

I went to the Bar-B-Que pit and retrieved a wire brush, then to the shed for a quart of motor oil. I brushed the steel door until the rusty steel shown with an iron oxide red. I dowsed the hinges with an extra liberal dose of motor oil. Then I wire brushed the Brass lock. It brushed up with surprising ease and shown with its quality in the afternoon sun.

The day had been a long one, and the oil needed time to soak through the rusted hinges before the door would ever consider swinging open. The locks clasp was as thick as a kindergarten pencil. Trying to break it would be an effort in futility. I knew what lay ahead of me was a new pack of hacksaw blades and some sore muscles by the time I sawed through the lock!

The man in the mirror now had his proof positive he demanded. I owed Chucklehead an apology and I knew it! "Glad I've got a bucket full of coal… that should make things go some easier" I said to myself that evening as I loaded up the stove.

When the stove came up to a full blaze, I opened the stove door and thowed in two large lumps of coal. I set on the couch behind the coffee table with a fresh bottle of Jack Black and a tumbler.

I rimmed the glass with a double shot like only a riverboat gambler wise in his ways might do after taking the house. Normally, I'd go for the burn. Being well aware of possible unintended consequences… I only sipped at my liquor. I owed Chucklehead an apology, and apologies have never come easy for me!

Halfway through my drink came a rumbling from the belly of the stove. Then came a happy-go-lucky laugh that raddled all the way up the stovepipe. Ha ha! "Wefty… hey Wefty! Geezzz Dude! I been wondering what the dad gum heck happened to you? Are you pissed the dad gum heck off at me Wefty?"

"Not at all Chuck!" I replied. "Ha Ha… I'm sure gwad Wefty… You're the first fwend I've had in a wong wong time Wefty!"

"Chuck, the pleasure of being your friend is all mine! Please forgive me for disrespecting you the first time we talked." "No pwoblem Wefty, no pwoblem! Polks have a hard time taking me seriously with my peach impediment and all."

"I thought when I died, my tongue would quit being twisted, but no such wuck, it's bounded up just wike its always dad gum been. Polks have always made pun of de way I talk, dat's why dey call me Shucklehead. Haha!

"Hey Chucklehead, you in the mood for another chunk of coal?" "Geezzz Wefty… taught you'd dad gum neber ask! Hee hee!

Upon his reply I tossed a nice chunk in the open door of the stove. When I did, the flame turned gas stove blue and he wafted out of the door on a flame. For the first time I saw a toothless grin stretch all the way across his wavy face. "Haha! Cheers Wefty!"

His smile was as infectious as his eyes were kind. With a "Salute!" I tossed back the tumbler and just like Chucklehead, I got the Burn!

I would come to know that Chucklehead knew his coal like I know my whiskey.

Just like my favorite whiskey is Jack Daniels Black

Label… his favorite coal is Anthracite. Just like me, Chuck will settle for Lignite if that's all that's available.

Bituminous coal gives him a hangover, like Southern Comfort does me!

I closed the stove door and went to raid the refrigerator for last night's leftovers.

Luckily, I hadn't throwed my back out scraping moss. Still, I felt the tiredness that comes with a hard day's work. I crumbled a couple of corn fritters in a Jethro bowl of pinto beans and set at the kitchen table enjoying the extra flavor beans have to offer, after the spices and seasonings have had a chance to marry in the refrigerator overnight.

Jazzy sat to my left in eager anticipation knowing once I'd shoveled down enough to knock the edge off my own hunger, I'd dole her out a portion. Even though her doggie bowl is always full, she wants whatever I'm having.

After dinner, I retired to the living room and set for a spell in my rocker, letting my food settle some before I did what Kory always called… getting horizontal.

Just before my nightcap, I stepped out on the front porch to take a whiz and check the thermometer… 31 degrees… According to the Farmer's Almanac, that's about four degrees lower than was predicted for early November. Somebody needs to Bitch Slap that frickin' weatherman!

There's a new moon tonight, and even though the

shadows are deep, I have too much to be thankful for, to waste any heart beats on that gal-dern weatherman.

I walked toward the water tanks still feeling all the relief that resolution has brought me in better understanding the nature of things. From that vantage point I could breathe crisp Kansas air while encompassing all the good fortune life has blessed me with.

I had Jazzy, and a warm house for us to sleep in. It's good to know my house has all that is needed to make a home, Kory showed me that... even though it's just a house without her here. I had my social security check, the truck patch, and a little music money to make my way with. I had Daddy's Martin D-28 that has an intrinsic value beyond the value of money.

Ole Blue could be bought for a price, but the buyer better have a suitcase full of hundred-dollar bills!

I watched the windmill bird dog the icy wind like a weathervane. The monster blade caught every breath of breeze like a greedy miser. A great gust came rushing across the shorn flat prairie and sent the windmill flying! Dressed only in long johns, it sent my sock feet flying back toward the porch as well!

Once inside, I made a bee line for the stove. I held out my hands soaking in the warmth. With the timidness of a hungry child, I heard Chucklehead ask just above a whisper. "Wefty...hey Wefty... you got another shunk of coal?"

Barely able to contain my laughter I said. "Sure Chuck… I'm fixing to have a night cap. Think I'm going to have a double shot… you want two chunks? Hee-hee! Don't dad gum mind if I dad gum do! He-he! Geezzz Wefty… you dee bestus dad gum friend dis ole ghos eber had!

FIFTEEN

The next morning Jazz and I were setting in the parking lot at Chalmer's Hardware when the "OPEN" sign began to flash. I went straight for the tool section.

Now that I'd embraced my new reality about the existence of parallel universes, shadow people, bigfoot and the here-after. After coming to terms with the undeniable truth that there is in fact a ghost living in my stove? My nightmares had disappeared!

I've always trusted my dreams. Many are the songs I finished writing in my sleep.

That magical third verse that came in the night when my sixth sense was tuned into the either. When my synthetic imagination was asleep with the rest of me. When my creative imagination was first mate... and my subconscious mind took the helm. Only in my dreams have I ever been able to write beyond my own ability.

In my dreams last night. I saw myself at the end of the day in defeat...the lock on the secret door had defeated me! Try as I might, the hacksaw handle only raised blisters on the palms of my hands, though I had barely scratched the surface on the well-made lock.

Worse yet, was when I slipped the timeline continuum and saw into the future. The blood on my guitar neck told me all I needed to know about playing Mayor Talby's birthday party. Last night's dream saved me... I awoke this morning with a brand-new plan!

I walked past the hacksaw blades like they weren't even in stock! Down past the Skill Saw display I found just what I was looking for. A four and a half inch Ryobi Disc Grinder. It was the same shade of blue as the one in last night's dream.

I studied out the selection of attachment blades. I chose three cutting wheels for the lock, and one grinder disc to sharpen the lawnmower blade with.

Cutting the lock would be a one-time thing, but having a handy way to sharpen the lawnmower blades would come in handy from now on.

After the sale of my Halloween pumpkins, and the check Judge Harris had awarded me for wrongful detention, I was funded well enough to buy the necessary tools to make the job of opening the secret door go more easily.

I carried the Ryobi to the check-out counter along with a propane torch to heat the rusty hinges with. Along the way I bought a pair of leather gloves and a grinder shield for eye protection. As I meandered in the check-out line waiting my turn, I spotted an end-cap display heaped with a variety of extension cords. They were on sale, so I picked up an extra heavy duty 50-footer. That way I knew for certain I could reach the third water tank from the front porch plug-in.

On my way home, it occurred to me that I hadn't mentioned to Chuck last night about finding the secret door. Nor did he bring the subject up either. Our conversation was minimal, unlike the night we'd first met. Last night's encounter for me was a chance to apologize to Chucklehead. For Chuck, it was a chance to except my apology. We were both glad to let bygones, be bygones.

Previously, what might be found hidden behind the secret door had never been an issue. I thought the only reason Chucklehead mentioned it in the first place was to prove his own existence. Proof positive that along with the train station's antique stove, I had inherited an even older ghost.

After finding the hidden door yesterday, and having a bedtime toast with Chuck last night, today my curiosity has my mind jumping like a jack rabbit!

As good dogs oft times do, Jazzy had read my mind. When I opened the truck door on our arrival, she hightailed it to the water tank and leaped up on the pile of moss for a ring-side view. She waited patiently while I gathered extension cords from the lawnmower shed and stretched them as far as they would reach. With the new 50-footer, I had just enough.

Sparks flew like the Fourth of July when I lit into the old lock with my new Ryobi grinder! In no time at all, it lay smoking on the ground. The hasp however, refused to budge. I'd oiled all three hinges yesterday but had overlooked the hasp.

Knowing that patience is a virtue, I oiled the hasp and set off to gather eggs and feed the chickens. The girls were huddled by twos and threes in their nesting boxes sharing warmth. The porch thermometer read 19 degrees when we left the house this morning.

I broke ice from their watering trough, filled my hat with eggs, and headed to the house for a fresh cup of coffee and to warm up. The wood stove was still putting out a fair amount of heat but had burned down to embers from early this morning. It was time for another round of stove wood.

I'd never seen Chucklehead by the light of day before. I didn't know the first thing about ghosts except that one lives in my stove. I'd come to terms with the fact that the Spirit is what's left behind, when the flesh is gone.

I didn't know if ghosts were like vampires who only come out at night? I thought about throwing a chunk of coal in the fire just to see what might happen… but I thought the better of it.

I'd begun to study my Bible a lot after Esmeralda and her Ouija Board. After Chucklehead and the poltergeist and all. The Bible speaks plainly about the Holy Ghost.

The poltergeist showed me that a Spirit doesn't have to be Holy to be a ghost, that's for damn sure! Just because you're a ghost doesn't make you Holy either! The only ghost I've met so far that wasn't a pure-dee-asshole, has been Chucklehead!

After I'd finished my coffee and bumped up the fire, I opened my toolbox in the spare bedroom that I used mostly for storage. From the toolbox I pulled my flat clawed framing hammer, bought from Jeter Pawn to replace the kitchen floor.

With tools in hand and Jazzy tagging along beside me I stopped on the front porch to read the thermometer. The egg yoke yellow sun had brought the temperature up to just below freezing.

I swung the framing hammer hard against the chisel wedged tightly behind the hasp of the secret door. My efforts produced no results at all, except making the cold chisel ring like a church bell. I set on the edge of the slab trying to figure what to do next, when I remembered the propane torch.

The motor oil smoked until the hasp began to glow red. Then a few light taps on the chisel wedged the hasp open. I dug the hammer's claw between the door and its heavy steel frame, hoping yesterdays' oil had penetrated the rusty hinges enough to loosen them. I pulled hard on the long hammer handle with all my might. After a few hard tugs, I heard the hinges begin to creak. With another good dose of motor oil, the door was soon swinging freely!

When the door first opened, a heavy musky smell came tumbling out. It was an odd smell, one that affected my olfactory and made my senses keen. The smell was both fresh and putrid simultaneously. It reminded me of cucumbers mixed with the smell of death. Soon, I became accustomed to the delightfully putrid odor and disregarded it, but Jazzy didn't. She stood at attention with the hairs on her neck hackled and her eyes ablaze.

After shushing her, I Looked down in the deep dark cavity with disappointment. All I could see on my first inspection, was a large canvas chute that in my best assessment, was used to funnel water into the boilers of those mighty iron horses that ruled the rails of yesteryear.

I was just about to reach down and pull the monstrosity out of the tower leg when I heard a mild explosion! I looked up in time to see a shower of sparks and suet boiling from this year's new stove pipe! There was Chucklehead riding on a clean blue flame just outside the weather cap... his smokey white beard must have been three feet long.

"Wefty!... Wefty... WEFTY DON'T!" Feeling most

beside myself, I grabbed Jazz up and headed for the house. Ashes were still floating to the ground when I made the front porch.

"What the fuck just happened Chuck?" I demanded! "Hey man… sorry Dude!"

Chucklehead replied. "You trying to burn the house down or what?... Answer me!"

Chuck started stuttering uncontrollably. "Heck ma ma man! Guess I should'a dad gum told ya'… dat ole tower legs been plum full-a rattle-moxigans long as I member! It's a dad gum good thing I peepeded out the chimney when I did! I've seen water tenders go for that slicker you was fixin' to fetch out, an neber come demselves back no mo… not even to draw der pay!"

"Let me get this straight Chucklehead. You told me about the third drippy leg the on third water tank with the secret door in the concrete support covered in moss, but you failed to mention it was full of frickin' rattlesnakes?... why's that? You looking for a roommate or what? That damn stove might get a little close for the two of us don't you think?"

"Pwease forgive me mer Wefty… I dad gum should'ah told you! I'll neber dad gum put you no mo in harms way… you can take my word on dat… even if I am just a dad blame ole goas'!

My blood had come down some. I was yet to figure what to do with a rattlesnake pit 150 feet from my front door. For the time being, I couldn't help but laugh in the hilarity of it all! When I can erase the image of ole Chucklehead's face in a shower of sparks with his beard hanging down, then maybe I'll know where to begin.

"Hey Chuck! I could use a double shot! What about yourself?" "Haha! Don't dad gum mind if I dad gum do, dare Wefty! Hee-hee!"

I tossed a couple of coal chunks in the stove for Chuck and poured a couple of shots in a tumbler for myself. "Cheers Chuck!" I said on my way back out the door. I heard the stove rumble with a happy salutation as I pulled the door two.

Now that I knew to proceed with caution, I backed Ole Blue up by the water tank leg and fastened a "C" clamp attached with a tow strap to the rubber slicker. I yanked a knot in the tow strap and looped it around the bumper hitch. Then I fired Ole Blue up and snatched that sucker right out the secret door! Half a dozen Diamond backs slowly slithered out of the slicker. They were big and cold and slow. My garden hoe was right there on the slab. I picked it up and made quick work of them.

Even though the rattlers were half asleep in hibernation, they were aware of the intrusion. As I peered down on them with my Mag-Lite, they set up an eerie witchdoctor roar with their hideous tails shifting from side to side and rattling like castanets.

I gazed in a state of fear and amazement as they rolled like a fresh can of worms tumped over on the riverbank. Forked tongues flicked in the air through open mouths with heads flattened and fangs showing. Their numbers must have ranked in the dozens!

I watched as they slowly slithered through their own excrement toward the four black walls of their den. Beady eyes shown with purpose as they tried to climb up toward me.

Slowly the tangled knot in the center of the den came untangled revealing what appeared to be a small but sturdy arch topped chest. The chest, like the secret door, looked like it was held together by rivets. Though it was covered with snake shit, I could see the uniform spacing that can be seen only in the craftsmanship of a boilermaker.

Slithering through their own excrement they tried to climb the slimy walls but could not. Their continuous rattling brought them all together in solidarity. Their uniform message was clear... we dare you!

Overtaken by what I'd just witnessed, I slammed the secret door shut and put the cold chisel in the hasp where the lock used to be, just for good measure!

That evening I loaded up the wood stove and threw in a chunk of coal for Chucklehead. It wasn't long before I heard his usual salutation. "Ha ha! Hey Wefty!"

"Hey Chuck! You know anything about that chest in the snake pit?" "Yep... Sure do!

Say Wefty... you wouldn't have another chunk of coal handy, would ya?" Hee hee!

"Oh, I see how you are now Chuck! Got a bit of conn

in ya, do ya? Next thing I know you'll be wanting Anthracite!" Hee hee... don't tease me like dat Wefty! Christmas is coming next month though... you know? Hee hee!

"What's in the arch topped trunk Chucklehead?" I asked impatiently. "Give me just a dad gum minute Wefty. Don't you ever kween dis dad gum stove out? I'm in ashes up to my dad gum ying-yang!"

With that, Chucklehead turned into the Tasmanian Devil in the belly of the stove and set up a swoosh that made the stovepipe raddle with a sound like gravel being sucked up from the floorboards at the carwash. Out from the rain guard came an ash grey cloud from the stovepipe that headed toward the windmill's big blade that was bird dogging a light breeze.

"Whew... dat's better! Ole Shucklehead don't mind no coal ash, but that dadblame wood ash dad gum chokes me down so I can't talk! Thow me another chunk of coal if you doesn't mind Mer Lefty... sose I can catch my breath some. Then when I dooze...

I'll tell you about Ballam's box."

My intention was to stay in control of this conversation, yet I was not succeeding. I had been manipulated by Chucklehead yet again! It's not that I mind giving him all the coal he wants... it's just how he conns me out of it! I guess it hurts my pride some to know that a dad gum ghost can play me like a pinball machine!

I open the stove door and throw in a chunk the size of my fist, then turn up the Jack and drink straight from the bottle… like I needed the burn to console me… and maybe I did?

I rocked in my rocker while Chuck was supposedly catching his breath. It crossed my mind that this could be just another chess move for Chucklehead. In the silence I set there like a pompous pool player slowly coming to the realization that he'd been taken in by the cunning persuasion of a Bona fide pool shark! I was behind the 8 Ball. There was nothing I could do but wait until he caught his breath. Hopefully then, he would tell me about the arched top trunk and its owner… Ballam.

"Haha… tanks Wefty! I appreciate that big ole lump of coal! It queered out eberything that was dad gum aggravating my dad gum ole peech impediment.

Here's about Ballam. Ballam was a witch. He come from witches, so they ain't no way he'd be different fruit, from the dad gum tree he fell from… that wouldn't make a lick a' sense!

What's more is dat Ballam was stole from de witches as a shild. He came up making blacking ink pots in a print shop called Southern Illustrated News. Dat was up Virginia way where dee witches is thick as sweet on honey!

Ballam, he got wise about slavery setting type at dee newspaper as an indentured servant. After his servitude,

Ballam struck a bee line to New York City, and took up right off with Harper's Weekly.

Ballam was white as roses are red, but he knew it weren't the color of a man's skin what made him a slave, it was the greedy hearts of Soul-less men who held their own comfort above a hundred other men's agony.

Ballam came from de witches, so if he had a soul at all, the best he could hope for was to get his ticket punched for a non-stop straight for hell! He'd come from the cradle with his back against the whip. That's why he was hard to put up with if you were a friend of Ulysses S. Grant, and he knew I was."

I set rocking in my chair and listened to the story that Chucklehead told. Evidently, getting rid of the wood ash had done him a world of good. I could understand his every word. We'd engaged in conversation enough that his impediment had become a dialect to my ears. Besides, he'd been dead longer than I'd been alive. What gives me the right to judge!

"I hate it that Ballam went through all that Chuck, but what does it have to do with the arch topped trunk in the snake pit?" "Well it does dad gum it! I ain't used to talking this dad gum much, Wefty… got anymore coal? Hee hee!

I threw in a couple more chunks of coal as I settled in my rocker and knocked the poison off a brand new fifth of Jack Black. "Okay Chuck, what's in Ballam's trunk?"

By daylight, every window in the house was open. The old potbellied stove was glowing like a Halloween pumpkin and the house was hotter than the Fourth of July, even though the porch thermometer read 16 degrees the next morning at daylight!

Chucklehead told tale after tale about Ulysses S. Grant. About battle plans he was privy to as they were discussed with high-ranking statesmen and military brass. Because Chuck was a chucklehead with a speech impediment, his intelligence quotient was discounted to K-9 status by everyone except Ulysses.

Chuck was stoked on coal, and I was drunk on whiskey, so I don't know how much fact was in his fiction, or how much fiction was in his fact. I was too drunk to know the difference anyway!

Chucklehead knew so much about West Point; you'd think it was his alma mater.

Chuck talked about meeting Robert E. Lee and how even though they he and Ulysses fought on opposite sides in the Civil War, they fought side by side in the Mexican American war.

He told about how Ulisses kept a barrel of whiskey outside his tent at Fort Donelson, and how his constitution was strong enough to stay away from it while important decisions in battle strategies were at hand.

He talked about what a drunk Jefferson Davis was, and told stories about some of their weekend benders they survived when both of them attended West Point. Chuck told about Fredrick Tracy Dent. Chuck said he and Tracy got on like Kings when he and Ulysses traveled back and forth between Point Pleasant and Fort Monroe. Chuck spoke of what chums they were. Such good friends in fact, that Ulisses married his sister!

Chuck talked about Rutherford B. Hayes and what a scoundrel he was. He talked about "Chief," the telegraph agent at the train station, and how upset he would get when the news came across the wire about reconstruction. He would spout Ex perlatives a mile long when he heard that Hays was rounding up the Indians and sending them to reservations.

And how Hamilton fish, Secretary of state, was all about reparations.

The Civil War ended in 1865 and Chuck didn't see Ulysses again until 1867 when he was appointed to be Grant's personal porter on his presidential campaign trail that consisted of speeches given from the train's caboose, mostly.

Chuck knew all about General Grants delectable delights when it came to food and drink, and how he demanded they be cooked, and served. The General had his own cookbook that he'd personally altered to his exacting standards. Penciled in notations as to the amount of this seasoning or that.

When it came to his stakes, Ulysses wanted only "T" bone. He drew an arrow toward the only cut of beef that suited his pallet. In parentheses he had written in capital letters: (RARE!)

I asked Chuck about the battle of Gettysburg up in Pennsylvania. Chuck got really quiet, then he said in à solum tone. "Mr. Grant took me into his confidence on the train one night after he had drunk himself sober. It was the only time I'd ever seen the General cry. If it's all the same to you Wefty, I'd just as soon not speak of it. After that, the stove cooled down, and Chucklehead never spoke another word the rest of the night.

I went around and closed all the windows because a chill was settling in fast. Then I stumbled to my bed and crawled in beside Jazzy with my question still not answered. "What was in the arch topped chest?"

CHAPTER
SIXTEEN

I went for the extra strength Tylenol before I even put on coffee that next morning.

Just as I poured my first cup, the phone rang. It was Doctor Fred, my chiropractor.

"Hey Lefty, you ready for tonight?" "Hey Doc… what's up?"

"Mayor Talby's birthday party! That's what's up!" (Amid all the strange changes that had happened since Doctor Fred last adjusted my back, I'd completely forgotten about the gig.)

"Oh yeah man! I stretched a new set of guitar strings last night! Put me in Coach, I'm ready to play! What time is sound check?"

"Be at the Community Center at seven, Lefty. Bring all the mics and cables you can round up! The Preacher from over at Whitwell is bringing his Telecaster, and

Warren Stinson Is bringing his Strat.

We got Deanna Deville on bass, and Ellis Williams on drums, me on the sax, and you playing rhythm and singing… we're going to blow the top off that place tonight, Lefty!" "Damn right Doc … See you at seven!"

I broke the Ice out for the chickens without bothering to collect the eggs. I knew the evening was going to be a long one, so I drank another cup of coffee and went straight back to bed once Jazzy had been looked after.

The soundman was a silver haired no nonsense kind of fella who had recently bought out "Jeter Music," up on Town Square. Doc said he'd turned knobs for the best in the biz, and that he'd wholesaled all the Grand pianos to make room for a full production recording studio in the back of the store.

The extra cables and microphones I'd brought along at Doctor Fred's request were not needed, far from it. The soundman had set the stage with a sound system fit for a concert hall! The Community Center had a maximum capacity of 750 people, but the sound system would have rocked Woodstock!

Phantom powered microphones with their cables laced down the boom stand to the stage floor, were then covered with mats to prevent damage or a trip hazard.

We were all a little (Awe Struck) with the extravagance, but no one more than Ellis Williams when the silver haired sound man (miked) his symbols and triggered his drum kit. You couldn't have taken the smile off his face with a Louisville slugger, yet at the same time, you could have knocked him over with a feather!

As the silver-haired soundman put us through our paces, banquet tables were being skirted with the red, white and blue ruffles of a Mayoral campaign. Elections were less than a month away.

Mayor Talby was very popular with the town's people. He had his finger on the pulse of the prosperous little agricultural community, that from its founding, had rejected the mundane, thereby capturing the lucrative assets of becoming a tourist destination as well. This made his re-election war chest, fat as a corn-fed sow.

I was enthralled with the smells that came bursting through the double stainless-steel doors when they were propped open with folding chairs. From the kitchen came an army of wait staff from the catering company. Huge portions of delectable delights were marched single file and placed in an obviously organized order with a roast beef butt, placed at the end of the buffet table soaking in azure. After overindulging in liquor last night, I suddenly realized I hadn't eaten since breakfast the day before.

"Pardon me sir!" It was the soundman. He stuck his finger in my belt loop and without the slightest effort, spun me around and slid an electrical device on the waistband of my Wranglers. "Here, put this in your ear." He handed me what seemed to be a very fancy ear bud with a wire loop that encircled the back of my right ear to hold the thing in place.

I heard a series of beeps that sounded like Morris code until he pushed a button on the mixing board. "Can you hear me now," he asked from his lapel microphone. I nodded in affirmation. "Good... address your microphone and sing "Mary had a little Lamb!"

I was somewhat taken aback at his request, but I did as he'd instructed. The sound in my ear was so clear that I started playing with my falsetto, and bluzing things up a bit. Just when I started really getting into it, his voice came across my ear monitor: "You're good!

I watched as every band member was fitted with an ear monitor. We were all seasoned musicians, but this seemed like the first day at school! The drummer, Ellis Williams was fitted with two such devices. The second of which was "Doctor Beat." It was a device that had been pre-programmed to the standard tempo for every song on our set list. It kept him steady all night. Neither running away with a beat, nor falling behind. The (Kick Off) on every song was right on time!

Warren Stinson was a little perturbed with the silver headed soundman when he turned every knob on his 1964 Black faced Fender Deluxe Reverb. You could see it all over his face, until he did a Clapton lick, and found that illusive tone he'd been looking for all his life!

The first song on our set list was, "Can't You See." By the Marshall Tucker Band.

Ellis Williams counted us off with his newfound friend… "Doctor Beat." We played all the way through to the end with a big crescendo, as the silver headed soundman made a few final adjustments.

The waitstaff and caterers applauded with admiring enthusiasm. Mayor Talby with arms spread wide, addressed us from the dance floor. "You fellas sound great! Thanks for coming to my birthday party and bringing your awesome combination of talents with you! I want y'all to drink plenty this evening… everything is on the house. All I ask of you is to get a good belly full of food first!"

Starving artists in the main, can be a seedy bunch. We permeate a society that chooses to feed us on their good days… so that they have someone to admire for our tenacity. On bad days, they still feed us, so they have someone to criticize for being so tenacious!

Even though the lot of us are a bunch of, "has been's, who never were," we all knew enough not to invite a banjo player to a "Rock & Roll gig, or to talk with your mouth full.

Smiles they were a-plenty even though few words were spoken. Everyone must have been just as hungry as I was!

Ellis Williams was the first one to break the silence. "Man Dude… I love the way those triggers make my drums sound! I don't know what that soundman did, but I'm addicted!

Just as everyone was pulling back from the table and wiping their mouths, The silver headed soundman came over to our table and introduced himself.

"I'm J.B. Baker." We all stood in admiration of the silver-haired soundman's accolades and expertise. One by one, we shook hands all around.

"Here's how this is going to play fellas. J.B. spoke with the tone of authority, like the varsity coach in a homecoming huddle.

"I recorded, "Can't You see" on your sound check. At eight p.m. sharp, I'm going to pump up the volume and play that recording."

"Drummer... once the music starts, set behind your drums and fall into the rhythm. Bass man, excuse me... woman. Strap on your bass and pick up the bass line. Preacher... you are preaching your sermon on the mount tonight... make it count Son! Singer, you're last on stage because you're the "front man."

Everybody, take your time making your way to the stage. Strap on your instruments and twin your own part in the song. Now guys, the overall intention in this type of introduction is to make your years of dedication look like it's merely child's play. Like making music was stamped on your butt when mama counted ten toes and ten fingers. Actually, y'all ain't half bad, but I'm going to make you sound like Honky Tonk Heros tonight.

Quicker than three shakes of a paralyzed lamb's tail came the sound of Ellis' drumsticks, setting the tempo for our sound check song the soundman had recorded earlier.

The place was already near full house capacity. People were lined up on both sides of the smorgasbord filling their plates with Mayor Talby's good natured way of buying votes.

Ellis Williams sauntered up the steps, stage right, strutting like a peacock.

Deanna Deville pranced up the steps, from stage left. She strapped on her bass with the confidence of a riverboat gambler. The Reverend was hot to play anything but "Amazing Grace!" I watched as he strapped on his Telecaster and bent his knees like a rocker. The Lord was just gonna' have to forgive him for tonight!

I stood slowly from the table and snugged down my Stetson like a Rodeo cowboy. Much to my surprise, a mild roar of applause went up when I did. Later that evening looking out over a sea of cowboy hats, I realized most of these folks had put bread in my tip jar before.

As the recording played, I addressed the microphone, and matched the pitch of my live voice, to my recorded voice. With sleight of hand, the soundman slowly blended the recording into live music! It was on like Donky Kong!

Never had I sounded more like George Strait, or George Jones. It would have probably killed my buzz had I known the silver haired soundman, was sending my vocal signal through a "pitch bender!"

Nevertheless, when we gathered up in the back parking lot at break, passing the break time joint. It was easy to see that to the man, everyone's head had swelled to a point that hats had been tipped back a bit for the necessity of comfort, or for the extrusion of genius that seemed to radiate from us all! Some admit it, others won't … but musicians are some of the kinkiest, most extravagant self-centered sombitches what ever drew a breath!

The night drifted away as we slowly approached the bewitching hour. That's when the band pulled in the reins and slowed the tempo for romantic couples to hold each other close and share a few "Tummy Rubbers." The dance floor filled up with sauntering cowboys both young and old, eager to get a fresh shine on their belt buckle.

Signs were posted on both sides of the sidewalk leading from the Community Center. They read: "No Alcohol Beyond This Point." Jeter's finest were positioned by trash cans provided for happy-go-lucky revelers, who happened to be too drunk to read the signs.

The band stood on both sides of the sidewalk receiving handshakes and hugs from one and all. Complements and accolades regarding their stellar performance abounded.

One young girl handed me a black magic marker and ask me to draw a heart around her belly button… then she asks if I would mind sealing it with a kiss? As bad as I wanted to do just that… I declined.

One by one, all the other musicians in the troop departed to destinations unknown. Warren Stinson was all but dragged away by what appeared to be twins, one on each arm!

The Sheriff's department lit out after their radio's started squawking like "One Adam Twelve." Just as I picked up my guitar case and headed for Ole Blue, I felt a hard punch to my ribcage with what my intuition told me, could be nothing but the barrel of a gun.

With a forearm strategically placed around my Adam's apple and my back painfully stretched against his pistol, I smelled the stale breath of a cheap assed cigar smoker who mumbled with the cold stub still in his mouth. "I told you, you son of a bitch! Now you're gonna pay!"

I was somewhat successful in breaking away from my assailant with elbows to his ribcage, until two thugs grabbed me while lard ass pistil whipped me. It was Kory Katz old landlord… the Pawn Shop broker.

SEVENTEEN

That night drifted in and out like a dreamscape as I regained consciousness. My first recollection was the comforting draft of warm air as it soothed my cold bones. I could taste the richness of warm salty blood as it trickled down my Frankenstein forehead and soaked my pearl snap shirt. I could tell by the feeling of mobility that wherever else I was, I was cramped in the floorboard of a fast-moving vehicle that showed no signs of slowing down anytime soon!

My left eye was already swollen shut, and my right eye wasn't far behind. I felt the car almost leave the ground as we traversed what I assessed to be railroad tracks.

Gravel pounded the fender wells for a mile or more until the vehicle slid to a stop. I could hear the two back doors open, then my own.

My neck popped and stretched, as two large hands pulled me from the floorboard with one hand under my chin, and the other hand around the back of my neck. Another set of hands grabbed me by my ankles. I was choking on my own blood as the two men picked me up off the ground and proceeded to toss me into what my right eye could still see, was a bar ditch.

They swung me once and swung me twice. I knew the third time would be charm. On the back stretch of the third swing, I heard the Pawnshop owner say; "wait! I'm not through with that son of a bitch yet!"

The henchmen stepped away and stood in the gravel laughing as the pawnshop broker lit a new cigar, then kicked me in the ribs until I rolled over the edge of the bar ditch. Then he said: "Win some... Lose some! Ain't that right Lefty?"

I was later to discover that Kory Katz had dawned a black wig and worked the door that evening. She was out to see if I was involved with another woman. And if the love she still longed to give me, had been lost to another woman's arms.

Kory had taken the job through a local temp agency. She had taken numerous videos of the performance from her stool at the door. After her shift with the Community Center had ended. She sat at a pic-nick table incognito shooting video of the band as garnered hugs and handshakes from all whom had attended, including a video of a vixen that persisted until Lefty drew a heart around her belly button.

Later, she told me that she wanted to cry as I held the Magic Marker. Then said she wanted to pull off her wig and run to me, when I declined to seal the young woman's belly button heart with a kiss.

Kory could tell that her Lefty was going home alone. She was just about to put her phone in her purse and run to me when she noticed the approach of two knuckle draggers, and her old landlord. Instinctively, she hit the record button on her phone, and caught the beat down.

Kory threw my guitar in her Jeep and gave chase. She blew through a red light in hot pursuit of the black Mercedes. Kory killed her headlights before crossing the railroad tracks. Then she shifted the Cherokee down in four-wheel drive and careened off in the bar ditch when the Benz slid sideways to a stop, on the gravel road.

She sat in the cover of darkness until the Benz spun around, and flew back toward the railroad crossing. Kory heard tires squalling as the Mercedes hooked a hard left on the black top. She threw a rooster tail as she made her way out of the ditch, and back up on the gravel road.

"Lefty! Lefty!... Lefty, she shouted! Kory heard no response. Frantically she searched along the shoulder of the road with her phone flashlight, until she found me!

The next thing I remember was waking up in Jeter Memorial three days later. When I came to, I was rethinking a roommate situation with Chucklehead. Even with Kory holding my hand and kissing my forehead, I knew I'd have to die, before I could even consider feeling better!

"Where's Jazzy?" Were the first words out of my mouth. "Don't worry Kory replied, I've been taking care of her, and feeding the chickens too. Everything's under control on the property. Your guitar is safe at home. Just take it easy.

The doctor says you're going to be fine. In a few more days you'll be going home. I'm going to take care of you until you can take care of yourself. Until then, I'm not going back to Kansas City.

Later that day I would find that Kory's video of my beatdown had already gone viral. Lerenzo Renaldo, the pawnshop owner, had already been apprehended, and sprayed down with D.D.T. by Marvin Gott.

Marvin, my beer drinking buddy at "Dance-A-Go-Go," slash, my jailer when I popped Ben Hoover up beside his nose, was one of my first visitors along with Lester Kramer. Marvin gave me the "down low," on my assailant. He was in trouble plenty!

CHAPTER
EIGHTEEN

Kory was a woman who held her cards close to her abundant bosom and played them well when the perfect opportunity presented itself. Her power of persuasion and seduction had taken her up the steps of the Capitol Building on the arm of "Speaker of the House" hopeful, C. Ray Wilson. What a scandal that turned out to be!

Wilson lost his wife of 18 years in the process, but Kory gained notoriety at the height of the, "Me Too Movement." Wilson was the first politician who had ended up on a downward spiral after coming under Kory's sensuous spell, but he would not be the last one.

Lefty had declared a few years earlier, that Kory was too young and pretty to be his widow, so she went back to Kansas City's Political circle where she used one politician after the other as a steppingstone toward her own social aspirations. Kory had become, "High Society." A social butterfly with a knack for showing up on the arm of whom ever was "Trending." As a result, Kory had become a "Media Darling." Even though it was I, who took the beating, it was she who made front page news.

Kansas City Social Light Saves Musician's Life.

My fourth day in the hospital was when my abduction and beating made the news cycle. As any politician would, Mayor Talby took full advantage of my unfortunate incident. As I lay propped up in the hospital bed with my head bandaged and my purple eyes showing, a camera crew from "The Kansas City Star" blinded me as they flashed pictures while Mayor Talby signed the cast on my broken arm, and Kory set beside me offering comfort.

Kory's tender lips made a mark on my cheek as she announced that Mayor Talby had invited her to a ceremony in Jeter Park. No explanation was needed when she brought me the Sunday paper.

Unbeknownst to me, I had become Mayor Talby's poster child in his new, "War on Crime!" There I was, in the newspaper with the mayor signing my cast. To the right of that picture was one of Mayor Talby presenting Kory with a Key to the city in honor and appreciation of her outstanding heroism and courageous selflessness, in the course of my rescue.

The doctor released me that following Wednesday. My face was still a mess, but I could see out both eyes again. Kory had cleaned my house to a point that it was almost unrecognizable. There were little bottles of perfume plugged into the wall sockets that made the place smell like Springtime.

Ole Blue was parked in his usual spot… in a matter of speaking. I knew without asking, that it was Kory who had driven him home from the Community Center. She did pretty good going forward as long as you were prayed up good and had your seatbelt on.

Her inability to backup, was one of our few points of contention. She'd cut the wheels the wrong way every time. I couldn't help but laugh when frustration overtook her.

Every time she tried to parallel park, I'd hold my mouth to quell my laughter, until snot shot from my nose. She would get mad as an old wet hen!

Blue was parked as if he'd been abducted by a UFO, then randomly dropped from a flying saucer by an Alien who'd obviously never completed an approved Driver's Education course.

Mayor Talby was reelected by a land slide. His "War on Crime" settled like dust after a thunderstorm. My beatdown was no longer in the news cycle.

Chucklehead was not news to Kory. She'd always known the train station was haunted, she just didn't know Chuck lived in the stove. Chuck had been aware of her, since Kory was a woman child when she'd build a fire for a warm place to make out in the abandoned train station after the cold of Winter had set in.

The first time I threw a chunk of coal in the fire, I ended up just going on to bed, I couldn't get a word in edgeways.

Kory went back to Kansas City at the end of November. Nursing me back to health had drawn us closer than we'd ever been. Chucklehead had become a part of Kory's life now, as well as my own. He had not taken from my well founded beliefs, but had only added to my understanding.

Knowing there is a life beyond this one, and that the door of death is only a portal leading into, "not another chapter, but a whole other book." Life after death is like a sequel with the main characters brought back on stage with an encore. Each character fulfilling his own destiny through eternity.

With the newfound wisdom I had acquired through all that had transpired, I ask Kory to be my bride forever more, and through the ages… Kory said: "YES!"

Her trip to Kansas City was not to go back to the social life that had been her second choice to the life she and I, had once shared, but to announce our betrothal, and load the Cherokee with all a country girl needs when she leaves her city self behind.

It took a few days to tighten up loose ends, but there

she was again, on December fifth with the Jeep loaded to the hilt.

It was reminiscent of the December fifth exactly four years earlier when her landlord had wanted her to pay up in ass. This time was very different, Kory wasn't running from anything, she was running to everything she'd always wanted.

At long last… Kory was home!

Kansas City Star ran another exclusive, but not on the front page this time. It was in the gossip column of the Society Section.

Kory Katz to Marry Assailed Musician.

The Columnist tried to play the story straight while getting in a few underhanded jabs that were carefully crafted to land just below Kory's belt. Incidentals just this side of slander in regard to Kory's scruples and moral standing, with an awkward slant toward her sanity. Kory laughed hardily as she read the article to me. She knew the gossip columnist well. "Sherry Salari lives in a glass house, but she's always the one to cast the first stone!"

CHAPTER
NINETEEN

Days of bliss like sweet dreams without number, seemed to pile one atop the other as Thanksgiving came with abundance. Every blessing that could be prayed for, was.

After the fourth Thursday in November had past, Kory diced the leftover turkey and made pot pies with a plethora of fresh vegetables and seasonings in her cream sauce that would take an Angel, half full of pie to describe!

By mid-December, our little wood framed house was decorated with such a festive Yuletide glow, that even the poltergeisters were thinking about turning over a new leaf. According to Chucklehead, some even spoke of heading for the light!

For most folks, alcohol consumption peaks through the Holiday Season.

I hadn't realized Jack Daniels had become my closest companion in Kory's absence. Now that I had her to hold, the burn of Jack Black took a backseat to the fire in Kory's kiss.

Holding her warm soft hand as we drifted through the cold hard nights of December had lifted the fog and revealed a better man in my sobriety.

Even Jazzy softened some, knowing the both of us had Kory's caring hands to pet her back, and scratch mine, as long as either of us had an itch to scratch.

You ain't never seen the like of pure dee perfection what come out of the oven that Christmas! A ham with pineapple circles nailed down with what Kory said was a cinnamon spice called, cloves.

The ham's Hyde had been brushed with brown sugar until it was tan as a Hula Dancer's cheeks. Candied yams and green bean casserole. A boat of ham gravy that would do any Irish potato proud, even if he were too poor to own his own pat of butter!

Pumpkin pie, with its alluring smell of nutmeg was so prevalent it mixed seamlessly with the sweet smell of cherry cobbler and apple pie. The cranberry sauce set by a sheet pan of brownies that had managed to get my hand slapped twice before we bowed our heads and said Grace that afternoon.

The evening was spent exchanging presents and sharing smiles and heartfelt hugs around the handsome holiday tree. The tree was a work of art all in itself. Kory had drooped it with deep weighty snows of garland and icicles. The star atop the tree almost touched the ceiling as it glowed above us, as though it were shining down on Bethlehem. I was in awe of its Majesty.

The new year would come with the revelation as to the contents of Ballam's box.

It was Kory, not I, who figured out how to extract the arch topped chest from the secret door of the third drippy leg of the third wooden water tank.

A six-foot step ladder would have worked nicely, had it not been for what Chucklehead called: The dad gum ole rattlemoxigans!

Even though nighttime temperatures plummeted well below the freezing mark, Geothermal conditions six feet below ground level registered in the low 60's. Ideal conditions for pit vipers during hibernation.

My first consideration was fire. Fire would kill the snakes alright, but might heat the metal chest to a point that would destroy its contents as well. Kory had a better idea… Dry Ice!

CHAPTER

TWENTY

We had a White Christmas that year with several other substantial accumulations of snow to be counted after the new year had arrived.

The Cherokee had four-wheel drive which might come in handy over in Smokey Hill as we waded through the bottoms along the river down toward the fish camp.

The fish camp used to be a Sinclair gas station. Their Logo… "Put A Dino in Your Tank!" Still stood stark and tall with the oil company's official prehistoric Mascot, on the weathered sign above the bubbling cauldron of minnow tanks that sent clouds of vapor rising toward a gloomy Kansas sky.

Cleatus Stinson, the proprietor, was salting down the sidewalk when we arrived. He hugged Kory and shook my hand, calling us both by name.

Cleatus was related to everyone in Smokey Hill, either

by lineage, or marriage. Warren Stinson, the local legend hotrod guitar player who got dragged off by twins after playing the mayor's birthday party? That was him, the very one, he was Cletus Stinson's great grandson.

There are people with a gift for remembering phone numbers. There are those who can tell you how to get wherever you're going from wherever you're at, off the top of their heads, including State Highways, Farm to Market roads, and interstate mile markers, and the best places to buy fuel, where to eat, and who serves the best cup of coffee. (Truck drivers mostly.)

Cleatus Stinson's Savant Syndrome centered around his innate ability to remember everyone's name, what they preferred for bait, what kind of cigarettes they smoked, or chew they chawed. What brand of beer they drank, and just how they liked their Bill Williams Hot link dressed.

The building he occupied was purchased when the Eisenhower administration put in the interstate highway system. Interstate 70 had drawn the life's blood from Smoky Hill, as well as many other little farming communities.

The bait shop was a gathering spot for locals who liked a friendly game of Checkers, a round of poker, or a fast-moving game of Dominoes. If you were over 60 and liked to talk about the weather, you were in the right place!

License plates had been pushed to the sealing and

nailed securely with a roofing tack in all four holes provided. Some dated back to the thirties. All fifty states were represented. The collection wrapped all the way from one corner to the next until it came all the way back around.

There were several tables randomly placed. They varied in size but shared a few things in common. Each table was draped with a red and white checkered tablecloth. Every table was round as a wire spool, because that's what they were, wire spools. Each table had a hole directly in its center that fit a Dollar General Store ashtray… perfectly!

I've never walked in the Fish Camp, what my mouth didn't water for a Bill Williams Hot Link sandwich. Cleatus served them on a single slice of "Bunny Bread." The slice of bread did little more than to keep your fingers clean.

The circumference of a "Bill Williams Hot Link," had a girth like a homegrown cucumber and they were longer than a whore's dream.

Behind the counter set two big oval crockpots. One was full of hotlinks ready to serve. The other was full of links getting acquainted and falling in love with a red Savery sauce so thick that it almost bubbled, but at the last second thought better of it.

A couple winter's back, I decided to try my hand at ice fishing. I thought the ice was surely thick enough to hold me, but I was wrong! The water was only knee deep, so I emptied out my boots and headed for the Fish Camp to dry out.

Me and Cleatus were setting around the wood stove when I ask him how he'd come by his hot link recipe. I was curious to know why he didn't call them Cleatus Stinson Hot links?

The old man took off his glasses and cleaned them with his apron. The road map wrinkles that covered his weathered face told an interesting story, the story of his life. Mr. Stinson's shoulders began to slump as he drifted back in time.

I'd never seen him without his glasses before. His eyes were blue as a deep pool of spring water, but not nearly as large as they were when you looked back through his round pop bottle lenses.

His demeaner told me he was somewhere between answering my question, or telling me to mind my own damn business. He put his glasses back on and looked at me squarely, then began to speak.

"I was born in 19 and 26 in the stockyards of Chicago. Pap worked on the killing floor for Swift & Company. The stock market crashed in '29. The great depression lasted until I was thirteen. Pap was might near dead by then, worn down by 14-hour days on the killing floor in Pack Town.

Pap hurt his leg but kept working anyway. His leg got so he could barely hobble. That's when they let him go.

I wasn't far from being old enough to go to work, so I lied about my age and went to work anyway.

Swift & Company put me on as a gut washer. I was the first in the process of washing hog guts that further down the line would be sausage casings. I was wet and covered in hog shit from the beginning of my shift, until the day was over.

Pap's leg hadn't gotten any better by the time I was legally old enough to work.

When I started to work, there were four of us, now there's five. My oldest sister, Jessee, two years behind me, and Sarah, four years behind Jessee. Then came Baby James, the newborn.

My mother's youthful face had warn hard against the struggle and worry of trying to make ends meet on the only income she had to work with… mine.

We were months behind on rent when they took me off the gut line and trained me in as a sausage grinder, that's where I met Bill Williams. Things took a turn for the better after that!

Bill Williams had a plan, but he needed a partner in crime. I turned out to be that very partner. Bill was all about the Union. He said our working conditions would improve and our wages would go up, if the union came in.

His favorite saying was: "There's a lot more of us, than there ever will be of them!" His words wrang true in 19 and 43 with the (UPWA) United Packinghouse Workers of America came to fruition.

After we reported to the timekeeper at the end of the workday, we'd have to line up single file and get shaken down for any meat, knives, etcetera in our possession that was not rightfully ours.

There were no second chances. You would receive your final pay, less damages, and escorted from the plant, and blacklisted in less than five minutes. No one in Pack Town would hire you after that!

Ole Bill Williams could put on a poker face he could… yes indeed… like they weren't nothin' to it! No one in the plant looked sourer and more downtrodden than that very man. He'd hobble around arched over all day every day until he gave me "The Sign." I'd be grinding hog scraps and trimmings right along, until from across the way he would bow up and smile. That told me all I needed to know.

I'd count down backward from a hundred, then I'd push fifty pounds of ground pork toward the chilling room and leave it in a line with all the other grinders carts.

(There were 22 of us.)

I'd walk down a narrow passage that was a service area for the chilling room, and piss down the rain pipe like all the other grinders did.

I'd wait for the chilling room man with his Eskimo coat and frosty beard to roll in another cart. Then I'd snatch a cart for me and Bill. I'd dump it down an access hole by the piss pipe. Bill Williams would catch it in a barrel lined with a burlap feed sack and carry it out back by the bone grinder.

I supplied the ground pork, Bill transported it home without a single suspicion, and Mrs. Williams seasoned the meat to perfection. She cased and bagged the hot links.

Little Italy bought every hot link sausage we made. Young as I was, and poor as my family was, I was more than tickled to be cut in for a third!

When the Union came in, Bill Williams went to work for the United Packinghouse Workers Union of America. My family would have ended up in the poor house had it not been for Bill Williams.

The hot links I make from scratch today are what saved my mother from an early grave. Jessee and Sara married well, and James got a college education, all because of Bill Williams. Bill died in the mid 80's.

Every time I sell a Bill Williams Hot Link, I'm proud to share his legacy, and his name. The man who saved my family from abject poverty, still lives on in every savory bite of a Bill Williams Hot Link. Does that answer your question, Lefty?

TWENTY-ONE

Kory slipped up from behind me, and blessed my cheek with a butterfly kiss, as I savored the last bite of my Bill Williams hot link. "I got us a six pack and a bag of chips for the ride home. They just loaded 30 pounds of dry ice in the Jeep. "She said.

Kory stepped back and studied me, then her eyebrows wrinkled with a question. "Are you okay Honey? Your face looks flushed, and your eyes look like you just woke up from a dream in Neverland."

"It's nothing to be alarmed about Sweetheart. I was just reminiscing about a story Mr. Stinson told me a couple years back, when you were in Kansas City, and I was Ice fishing. It's a good story. I'm surprised I haven't already told you... but I'll tell you on the way home, after we stop at "Mother Cluckers."

Kory always insisted on driving when we were in her

Jeep. She was smart, and good at most everything except for driving. We took Ole Blue most times, because Jazzy, as much as she loved her mama, didn't like riding with her... and neither did I!

On our way home, we slid through the Drive Thru at "Mother Clucker's Poultry Palace." Mother Clucker's deep fried chicken breasts were to Kory, what a Bill William's Hot link was to me.

As does usually happen, Kory pipes up and says. "Lefty, I'm really hungry for some "Mother Cluckers." Would you mind driving while I eat?" We swapped places in the Drive Thru as they prepared our order. As I slid behind the wheel, I glanced back a Jazz. She wagged her tail and panted in a show of conspiratorial solidarity.

As is the nature of most women folk, Kory would much rather talk than listen. I set the cruise control once we hit the highway and told the story Cleatus Stinson had told me about Bill William's Hot Links, all the way through, and without interruption. I could tell when she wanted to ask a question but couldn't... her mouth was full of chicken.

On our arrival home, I backed the Cherokee up to the snake pit. Kori and I had put together a game plan we both thought would work. First, I dowsed the creepy bastards with two five-gallon buckets of hot water. That was to wake them up... and boy did it!

A terrible stench went up as the hot water hit the snake shit! Their rattles went off as forked tongues flickered in the air as they slithered around trying to find something to bite. They tried with a vengeance to escape the hot water, but could not.

As they clung best they could to the snake shit covered walls trying to escape the hot watter, I dropped one end of the tow strap directly on the arch topped trunk. When I did this, they began striking the flat yellow nylon strap.

Some bit hard, but some of the biggest ones bit even harder. As they slowly came out of hibernation, their aggression was amplified by the concrete walls. Hisses could be heard above their orchestrated tails.

Their rattlers sounded like castanets in the concrete sound chamber. Fangs flashed like daggers as venom squirted, then hung in crystal droplets from their Ivory white surgical sharp instruments.

Kory had already flipped her wig. She'd snatched Jazzy up and went for the house.

I watched as the rattlers wrapped around the tow strap as if they were trying to choke it down. I almost shit myself, when one began to climb up the tow strap. Neither Kory or I had figured on that! That's when I threw all 30 pounds of dry ice right on top of the slithering bastards! A white smoke caused from dry ice meeting water, bellowed from the pit as I slammed the secret door and slid the cold chisel in its place, just for good measure!

When I came through the front door, Kory could see

that I was distraught. "You look like you could use a drink Lefty… you want me to pour you a shot?" "Maby later Darlin'… what I want right now, is a good hot bath!"

Next morning, I rose before dawn which was my usual. Kory loves her pillow more than I do. She'd grown used to a life of glamor punctuated with facials and pedicures and high thread count sheets. Things a well-kept woman, who is indeed well kept, acclimates to in no time at all.

The most expensive present I bought for her at Christmas was an engagement ring with a sprinkle of five small diamond chips. It wasn't much compared to the impromptu gifts of diamonds and gold she had acquired from aspiring politicians trying to garner a well yoked partner on their way up the ladder.

Kory said, "Diamonds and gold are a much better asset than a 20-pound bag of pinto beans." I told her, You can't eat diamonds and gold when things get hard." She tilted her head down slightly, then looked up at me through cat eyes and blinked. She pouted her luscious lips, then licked them sensuously. "The way I get my diamonds and gold, are when things… do… get hard!"

The most expensive gift I got for Christmas was a king size "Posture-Pedic Perfect Sleeper." I thought the mattress I had was just fine. I'd had it since I'd bought the property.

It was the best of the batch from the dozen that came when I bought the land. I pulled it out of the pile and put it up on shipping pallets where it could dry out. There weren't a single pee stain on it, and it had laid in the sun long enough for the bed bugs to have all died off. That was good enough for me!

Kory insisted that the Posture-Pedic was going to be our wedding bed, and that a wedding bed was sacred, if you was married by a preacher, and got the Lord's blessing and all.

I called the Fire Chief down at Jeter volunteer fire department. We talked about old times for a minute, and had a good laugh or two. I told him about My new mattress, and how I needed to get rid of the old one. He said I could go ahead and burn it as long as I didn't use car tires to get the fire started. We had another good laugh. We talked another minute more, then I dowsed the mattress with Ole Blue's last oil change and lit a match.

CHAPTER
TWENTY-TWO

When I came in from letting Jazzy out to do her duty and breaking ice in the chicken house that next morning, Kory was standing by the stove stacking me up a plate piled high with flapjacks. On the back burner, link sausage and thick sliced bacon sizzled in the cast-iron skillet, she always made too much, but I always got all I wanted. That was just Kory's way.

Anything we didn't eat, the chickens did. The rich orange color in the eggs they laid for us was proof positive that nothing went to waste in Kory's kitchen.

From pancakes to Blackberry cobbler and any pie you care to mention, Kory made almost everything from scratch. She said that just because a woman could take it up the ass, was no excuse to quit cooking for her man. She said men were easy to steal when their women got lazy.

Kory fed me breakfast, then we talked a while, but not about the weather. She licked the pancake syrup from my mouth, then we went back to bed for a while. What she wanted for breakfast wasn't on the menu.

I woke up on the Posture Pedic around 10 a.m. feeling like the perfect sleeper!

I was eager to find out if the dry ice had worked. I dressed for the outdoor temperatures and stole a kiss from Kory's lips on my way out the door.

Kansas can be gloomy in Winter, but on that day the sun shone like a polished lemon in a perfect cloudless sky. The porch thermometer read almost 40 degreasers, and the snow had melted just enough on its crust to make the snow crunch when you walked on it.

The windmill looked as sad and lonely as a man without a paycheck. Neither twig, nor branch, nor leaf did rustle. The air was as still and solemn as an old Judge with no one to approach the Bench. The windmill blades stood stark and still, as if they'd been carved in stone.

I had to spray a little starting fluid down Ole Blue's throat that morning before he would come to life. We were both getting up in years. After that day I started parking Ole Blue a little closer to Kory's Jeep, hoping that her Cherokee would do for Blue, what Kory had always done for me.

When I went to the third drippy leg of the third wooden tank where the secret door was, I was surprised to see the door frosted up so much that I could barely see the cold chisel in the hasp. The dry ice had worked! The door looked like a freezer that had long been neglected. I headed out to the lawnmower shed to collect the extension cords I'd run the grinder on when I cut off the lock on the secret door.

I had a plan that I would borrow Kory's hairdryer and defrost the door. When I got to the shed and loaded my arms with extension cords, I saw the propane torch I'd heated the hasp with. I hung the cords back on the wall and picked up the propane torch. I left the shed knowing I had a better idea.

By the time I got the metal door defrosted, Kory had come outside dressed like the Easter Bunny... she was fluffy from head to toe! The first sight of her made me feel like Peter Rabbit! I would have stopped right there and had my way with her, if I hadn't got my fill a few hours before. I dread the day she has to do me like I did Ole Blue this morning, spray ether down my throat to start me up!

Knowing better than to do it... I did it anyway! After the secret door was open, I put Kory behind the wheel and slid the other end of the tow strap on Ole Blue's bumper hitch.

"Just give Ole Blue a little gas Honey... then come up off the clutch nice and easy."

Well to make a long story short, Kory didn't know you had to push in on the clutch to make Ole Blue quit pulling. There I was, riding a chunk of frost covered rattlemoxigans down the pasture road with my feet flying in the air. and holding on to the tow strap like a rodeo cowboy holding a bull rope.

Kory panicked at first, then she let off the gas and hit the break until she choked Ole Blue down to nothing.

My Karharts were frozen to the rattlesnake infested chunk of ice, I had ridden for at least eight seconds. I'd already lost my cowboy hat, and was more than ready to bail… but my pants wouldn't let me.

Kory pulled my boots off so I could slide out of the Karharts. As I ran in my skivvies and sock feet through the snow, I could hear Korry laughing all the way! I stopped at the front door and hollered back a Kory… did we get the box… did we get Bellam's Box?

I was too cold and naked to wait for an answer, so I turned the knob and let myself in.

Even though the whole ordeal was a fiasco, the arched topped chest came out with the nastiest, prettiest cluster of Western Diamond Back Rattlers a person could imagine.

The frosty clump of rattlemoxigans froze hard as a rock every night, and thawed a little more every day. By the third day, the clump of frost had reduced in size considerably.

On the fourth day, what once was a frosty clump, had become so clear you could see right through it. The dry ice had flash frozen them.

Some of the vipers could be seen with their cotton

white mouths still biting the yellow tow strap, with their fangs protruding. You could count their rattlers right up to the button.

By the fifth day, the gradual thawing process, had turned the chunk of ice into a Glass Menagerie. Once the rattlers had been flash-frozen, Kory wasn't afraid of them anymore. Kory said that when she was coming up, her and Gramps used to cut their heads off, poke a knife in their butt holes, and split'em up their bellies to where their heads used to be.

She said that once they were skinned out, Gramps would cut them into nuggets, dredge them in egg wash and bread them up in flour.

Kory laughed like a schoolgirl as the distant memory came back to her. She said the shanty would soon fill up with old timers packing moonshine in trade for a belly full of snake meat.

She crossed her arms and got a faraway look in her eyes. She didn't have but a scant few fond memories from her childhood to tell about, but I could see that the snake fries were one.

"Gramps would set a cast iron pot on top of the coal stove. Then he would ladle it half full of hog lard. When the lard come up to just about smokin', Gramps would gather up a double hand full of snake meat and shake the flour off. When it hit the grease, the nuggets would sink to the bottom as the lard churned up in a fury. After not more than a minute, the snake meat would come bubbling to the top in a golden-brown state of perfection!"

"By the time the first batch came out she continued, there was a line of old farts holding one of the three metal plates we owned. Every time a batch would bubble to the top, Gramps would take a tea strainer and fish out another plate full. Every time he did, he'd take a slug of their shine for payment. The more rattlesnake he cooked, the drunker he got."

"I didn't have no # 40 rod to trade Gramps, so I always ate last. After everyone had passed out, I'd do just like Gramps and bread me up a batch if there was any snake meat left."

" Best I remember, Kory said with her head tilted slightly, rattlesnake was the first thing I ever cooked. I can't say for sure though, I probably wasn't much more than six, or maybe seven."

Kory's demeaner completely changed after she told me her fond memory. Evidently, It led to a memory she was not so fond of. She'd buried her brutal past so deep in her subconscious mind, that it may never have come bubbling to the top had it not been for the snake pit.

Kory fell to her knees and began to squall. I watched her as she did, not knowing what to do until she held her arms out to me. I fell down on my knees and met her embrace.

Her heart felt hug was one like I'd never experienced before or since. It was like holding a little girl who had just become a war torn orphan child, and was just now coming to terms with her loss.

Kory cried until she cried herself to sleep that night. I tried everything I knew to soften her pain, but nothing worked. I got out my bottle and slept on the couch.

Sometimes with a woman, you just never know... sometimes a man just has to step back and let them cry it out. I guess there's more than one reason men call them, "Baby."

My sleep was restless that night. I knew that Kory's shaken foundation was no fault of my own, yet somehow, I felt responsible.

The Afghan Kory kept draped across the back of what she called "The Sofa..." and what I call "The Couch," was severely lacking in every aspect of comfort!

I had to dig my toes into the loose woven yarn so my feet were covered. When I did, I'd have to lock my elbows to hold the covers over my head!

I guess all women know this intuitively. It must come packaged in their D.N.A. When Mama ain't happy... ain't nobody happy! Like it or lump it. If you're a man, who is a man... that's just how things roll brother!

Somewhere in the wee hours, I stepped out on the porch to make a yellow spot in the snow. The thermometer on the porch post told me that the "Farmer's Almanack," was right on par for the latter part of January.

I thought about the weatherman and how hard I'd

cussed him in the past for trying to freeze us all to death. I thought about how I should probably forgive the simple bastard, but that would all shake out to be an apology, and I don't do apologies well!

Being I had a driveway full of frozen rattlesnakes and was sleeping on the couch,

I decided to give the weatherman one more good ole, "down the road cussing" just for good measure!

I knew full well that I'd forgive him come Spring, but this was January. By Spring, I'd come up with just the right words to pray, but as for that night, I cussed him like a seasoned sailor with one stump and a pegleg.

CHAPTER

TWENTY-THREE

That damn weatherman had me so stirred up, that I was still cussing him as I banked up the stove. I opened the damper for the fire to catch up. When it did, I cut the damper by half and headed for my bottle.

I unscrewed the lid and took a good hard pull. Then I took another one, just soze I could get the burn. About the time I did, I looked over at the couch, and there was Kory.

When Kory saw that I had finally seen her, she came to me. She pulled in close and just held on for the better part of a minute, then she arched her back and looked me in the eyes. "I love you Mr. Fishburne!" she said matter of factly.

Kory took me by the hand and grabbed my bottle of Jack with the other. She led me to our bedroom where there were three scented candles burning. Kory knew how to set the mood for comfort.

I kicked off my house shoes as Kory slid into our king-sized bed. She leaned me against a mountain of satin pillows, then cuddled in my arms. I knew it was her time to talk… and my time to listen.

"I'm sorry I lost it this afternoon Lefty." "Well, that's okay Baby, a woman has a right to cry." "That's just the thing Honey, I never had a chance to cry for Gramps until today.

I hated Gramps back then. When he died, I hadn't even got my period yet, but I felt like anything but a virgin."

"You see, Lefty, Gramps come up on the Tennessee River at the foot of Suck Creek Mountain around Chattanooga. His ma and pa were dirt poor. I heard him tell the story so many times that I know it by heart. Gramps was one who would never let the truth stand in the way of a good story, but looking back now after living almost 43 years, I can plainly see that what he told about growing up was the truth mostly."

"Gramps never got much schooling. In his day, what mattered most was bone and muscle. He was twelve years old when prohibition came in. Gramps made it through the sixth grade, but that was the end of his education. After school let out for the Summer that year, his pa put him to work loading sugar on a mule's back, then leading the mule up Suck Creek Mountain on the back trails.

Gramps told of the moonshine still. He talked about men who wore creased trousers and buck shined shoes. Men who drove hot rod cars with souped up motors and hidden tanks to haul the shine.

They'd leave out on a run with sweat on their brow, then come back with their Fedora tilted back and cash money on the barrel head. They'd tell about how they out drove, out run, and outsmarted the State Police on their last haul.

The runners would saunter around with thumbs in their pockets all cocky like, and strut like a rooster when they got their cut.

His ma and pa bought acres and acres along the riverfront with the lucrative proceeds from what came to be a game of cat and mouse between the revenewer's and the Francis family.

His ma always said: "Once you hold a deed, you have the rights of a property owner, no matter where the money came from."

City slickers and pencil pushers didn't have much of a chance against a clan of folks who'd been running that mountain barefooted for generations. By the time Gramps was grown, the Francis family owned everything east of the Tennessee River all the way up to the "Wildlife Refuge up on Suck Creek Mountain."

When a deputy Marshall came poking his nose in where it didn't belong down in Suck Creek, It weren't long before he realized he was in the wrong place at just the right time to bait a catfish hole!

Hillbilly people are clannish. When you marry, that's the side of the family you fight on! It don't make a damn bit of sense, but that don't make no never mind either!

That was Kory's excuse for Gramps being who he was.

"Old enough to bleed… old enough to breed." That was Gramps take on the matter when it came to young girls.

I guess I got sold early. Gramps said he knew that I'd soon be on the verge, and there weren't no point in putting off the inevitable. He had a knack for justifying almost anything.

Gramps brought me up after Mom and Dad went down on a riverboat coming up the Mississippi from New Orleans. I was left in the care of my grandma who came down with pneumonia and died that next Winter.

Gramps always said it was about time he got his due. He'd tell his friends, "Why should he abstain from the just rights of raising me, when he knew all along that I would give myself away for free in the name of love anyway?"

"Gramps always said this as he sat me on some old man's lap who happened to have a little #40 Rod to share if he could touch my bottom. Needless to say, Grandpa always had a powerful thirst."

Kory continued to speak. "I was still cutting out paper dolls when my innocence was lost to the grandson of a notorious moonshine runner. His name was Topper, and his stock in trade was cocaine. Topper offered Gramps a dozen quarts of # 40 rod if he could take me on a run up to Atlanta. Gramps said no at first. Looking back now, I can see he was just trying to sweeten the pot. Gramps always drove a hard bargain. Topper came back from his car with a chrome plated pistol, and the deal was done. I'd never even kissed a boy before that night, much less a man with whiskers!"

"After being his, "Pretty Baby" for a couple of weeks, I understood exactly why they called him, Topper!"

"Topper was a brash young man who was scared of nothing or no body. He kept a revolver within arm's reach no matter where we went, even in the bedroom."

"Sex with Topper was like a rodeo." Kory continued. "He would put me on my hands and knees, grab my hair like a bull rider, and have his way with me."

"He rode me like he was riding in the National Finals. The louder I screamed, the harder he rode me! Topper had no mercy. Whatever hole he found first, was the first hole to take a pounding."

"When he finally took me home, the shanty had burned to the ground with Gramps in it. I was devastated... mortified! When I began to cry, Topper started screaming at me... "get out!" When I didn't, he opened my car door and sent me sprawling on the ground."

"Topper revved the motor and spun away in his

Firebird. All that remained standing on the property was the chicken house and the clothesline. The clothesline still hung with the last washing."

"Gramps took a bath once a month whether he needed it or not. He said Jesus washed his disciple's feet. He said if that was the way of it, clean feet should have clean socks. Gramps would cut a hickory switch in a quickness if he didn't have clean socks."

"I slept in the chicken house for the next three weeks until my thirteenth birthday. All there was to eat was eggs and Blackberries. I cooked the eggs in a cast iron skillet I'd found sifting through the ashes."

It was late Spring, and the Blackberries were beginning to ripen… All their tender parts had begun to soften… and so had my own! Just when I'd healed enough that my butt hole didn't feel like a pine knot anymore, I got my first period. Gramps didn't need his socks anymore, so I tucked them in my panties and bled on them.

After my first period I began to feel a hunger in the deepest part of me. I blamed it on Topper at first. I had a longing that only a passionate man could satisfy. It wasn't long before I knew that it was just the woman in me. Things happened really fast after that!

TWENTY-FOUR

Summer vacation was only a few weeks out when Topper stole me. When I showed up the next Fall to start eighth grade, not a lot was said about my absence the previous year with the demise of Gramps and all.

Little did anyone know I'd just spent the last three months in Kansas City doing nothing but smiling brightly, and being pretty.

I'd spent the previous summer learning how to work men over. I learned how to make them work hard for my affections. I'd have them down on one knee within a week or two. Their pockets were deep, their Gold was pure, and their diamonds would cut glass.

I was kept nicely. Every suiter was sure he'd found his Cinderella. After being treated with their every kindness, and taking every gift they had to offer, I would let them know on no uncertain terms, that their glass slipper just didn't fit.

I've already told you more than a man needs to know about the woman he has plans to marry. I feel bad on one hand, but on the other hand, I've been totally honest with you.

You see Lefty, every woman's heart is a treasure trove of secrets.

I was set aback by Kory's honesty. I leaned against the velvet pillows and held her evermore tightly. Her love radiated through me. Also, I felt her pain and the anguish that had tormented her since before she was a teenager.

"Your future is in front of you, not behind you," I told her. When I think about how you were forced to turn pain into pleasure just to survive it, that makes me angry! Love is not supposed to be that way!

I'll feel selfish from here on out knowing the lover you've come to be is to my benefit.

I wish I'd been your first, instead of Topper. I wish I'd been the first one to bring you to the powerful orgasms you share with me when we make love.

The first time we came together Kory, I fell in love with you! We went all the way around the world together. From there, sex with you has only gotten better!

"Yes, I remember that night like it was yesterday. You were playing at The Red Door over in Neaderville. You'd come through the drive-Thru at "County Line Liquor" for some cowboy killers and a six pack.

You told me that you liked to sing love songs, that you didn't know a single sole in Neaderville, and that a pretty girl to sing to, would make the night go easy! You handed me a twenty-dollar bill. When I gave you back your change, I scratched the palm of your hand, do you remember?

"Kory Darling... any man who is a man could never forget that! There you were, like a vine ripened tomato. Luscious and lovely, ripe and ready to be plucked from the vine... tender and juicy, delectable and delicious, savory and succulent!

The last two songs of my fourth set I played just for you. You were the only one on the dance floor. Dancing by yourself and glancing up at me with a "come on look" in your eyes. The drink you had waiting for me when I stepped down off the stage. Yes, I remember that night Honey... what man doesn't remember when he's been bit by the love bug for the very first time?"

Kory's tears had previously streamed down her cheeks from the telling of Gramps and his demise. Topper, and how he'd treated her like a love slave. How he had forced her to choose between the agony of rough sex, and the passion that sometimes comes from being ravaged.

The candles burned throughout the night as we feasted like hungry wolves until we finally had our fill and fell asleep in each other's arms.

Had it not been for Jazzy's whiney pee dance, I would

have laid up with the ravenous Hell kitten who by her own admission, turned out to be the death nail to every Kansas City politician who thought their political magnetism would be multiplied inversely... if only the illustrious Kory Katz was on their arm. I couldn't help but feel a certain amount of "sorrow" for those palm greasing, ass kissing politicians as I kissed the face of the Siren whose irresistible allure had drown them all in their own pitiful puddle of wealth and greed.

CHAPTER
TWENTY-FIVE

When the sun began to share its warmth that morning, I retrieved the arch topped chest that had finally gained independence from the vipers it had been thrown amongst by Ballam many decades ago. Alas, Ballam's curse was soon to be broken.

The truth within the chest beckoned for me to lift its masterfully handcrafted lid and expose the secrets therein.

There was yet another lock to be delt with, but it would show only the slightest resistance against the new Ryobi's cutting wheel.

Ballam was a witch. I will not be the one to prognosticate or deliberate the power of his potions. If you were to ask me straight out where I couldn't get around your question.

If you held my feet to the fire, I'd have to say that

Ballam weren't no slouch! I'd have to tell ya' that Ballam knew his business when it came to being a witch, or what Esmeralda called, a Warlock.

After I'd washed decades of slimy snake shit off the metal trunk, it began to take on a film of rust as soon as it started drying. According to Chucklehead, there was a cedar box that had gone missing while he and General Grant came off the campaign trail.

I was surprised to find that when I opened the arch topped chest, I found another box wrapped in burlap that had been soaked in bee's wax. I supposed it to be the cedar box Chucklehead spoke of. Kory watched with an equal amount of curiosity and enthusiasm as I cut through the burlap with my pocketknife, then put the box in her hands after the burlap incasement had been cut away.

Together we gazed in awe at what lay before us as she manipulated the jewelry box hasp with nimble fingers, and carefully opened the lid. The aroma of cedar mixed with the musty smell of parchment abounded. A well-worn leather binder incased the slightly yellowed pages of what the book's spine would reveal to be… Ulyssis S. Grant's personal cookbook.

Peeking out from the corners of the cookbook lay a slightly yellowed parchment with an incantation scribed in scholarly fashion.

To the left of the book was a Gold tipped fountain

pen, and to its side, a cork topped bottle of ink that had long since lost its luster.

To the right of the book was a pair of wire rimmed spectacles. Notations throughout the book showed a diligent effort to make sure he had communicated correctly to the Chef. What he wanted, and how he wanted it cooked. Circles and underlines and arrows made it plain that the measurements were precise, and were what his pallet demanded.

You've never seen a happier ghost, than Chucklehead was that evening! "Hee hee! Hey Wefty! … I can go to the light now," Chuck exclaimed rattling the stovepipe. Then the stove door flew open.

There he was, floating on a clean blue flame. His image was a much younger man with dark wavy hair. For the first time, I could see he was an Irishman. His beard was neatly trimmed, and his countenance was utterly joyful.

Kory and I set listening into the wee morning hours about the rivalry that had developed between Balam and Chuck.

The Civil War had turned brother against brother and friend against friend, the latter being the case betwixt and between the two.

Ballam would not concede to his defeat with the inauguration of Ulysses S. Grant. Instead, he used the mighty power of all his sorcery to befall Chucklehead with a spell that would follow him beyond the grave.

In a fit of tears that blazed like kerosene, Chuck told how Ballam had stolen the cedar box from the train's caboose, thereby driving the wedge of distrust between he and General Grant after the election.

Chuck told how Grant in a fit of rage, dismissed him as his personal porter. How Kansas City Southern demoted him back to a "boiler tender." His demotion would eventually account for Chucklehead's demise.

We had to open the doors and windows when Chuck told his heartfelt story. Tears poured forth in a sorrowful flurry that only added to the flame.

Chucklehead's Christmas gift was just what he had ask Kory for... a fifty-pound bag of anthracite. What Chuck called, "Blue Coal." After the overindulgence through the Holidays, His tears were like kerosene.

"Get a grip on yourself Chuck!" I shouted. You're going to burn the house down if you don't stop crying!" Kory soothed him down with her gentle nature until the red-hot stove turned back to its normal cast iron grey.

After Chucklehead had regained his composure, he told of the spell Ballam had put on him. Ballam was a strong witch, and his spells and hexes and potions were very powerful.

Ballam had cursed Chuck's Spirit to remain earthbound until the box had been retrieved from the pit of vipers, or reclaimed to ashes, or the dust of the earth. Only then could Chuck cross over to the light.

Even with those demands being met, there was yet

one other hurdle to overcome according to the terms and conditions of the spell Balam had cast. According to the spell, Chucklehead must return to the rightful place of his birth before he was free to go to the light.

Each condition of Ballam's curse was written out point by point on the gently yellowed parchment beneath the General's cookbook.

After hearing Chucklehead speak of it in full detail, and reading the parchment again, I stood from my rocker and addressed Chucklehead point blank. Rising Fawn Georgia? Is that where you have to go to cross over Chuck? Yep Wefty… Wrizing Fawn Georgia!

Kory began to cry those tears that women cry when tears of joy and sadness come together in a mix master that cannot be refined or defined without a cacophony of words mixed with female emotion that no man among the living would understand anyway.

I pulled Kory to her feet and drawed her up under my arm there by the wood stove. It seemed that Kory as well as Chucklehead knew the revelry that would break the early morning silence.

Three voices gathered to gather in unison as if we had rehearsed those five words a thousand times before. "Rising Fawn, here we come!" And so it was to be.

The three of us came to an agreement. We would load the stove on the truck as soon as we could make the necessary preparations.

TWENTY-SIX

There are always preparations to be made when you have livestock, even if it's only chickens. After coming to terms, we all had a nightcap and drank a toast to the journey.

I called down to the volunteer fire department that next day and got permission to burn.

I filled an old rusty burn barrel half full of stove wood, and burnt the whole passel of rattlesnakes to ashes.

Later that afternoon, Kory followed me in the Jeep to Poskey's Full Service where we dropped Ole Blue off for an oil change, then we headed out to the Fish Camp in Smoky Hill.

I needed someone to take care of the chickens and look after things while me and Kory took Chucklehead to Rising Fawn so he could go to the light.

"Hey Mr. Stinson!" I greeted, as Kory and I stepped through the Fish Camp door.

"Come here Kory Katz!" The old man came from behind the counter and caught Kory up in a hug. Then he put his hands on her shoulders and held her at arm's length. "Come here, let me have a look at you!"

"I know you don't remember, but I used to carry you on my shoulders when you weren't no more than knee high to a grasshopper! My... what a pretty woman you've turned out to be, Kory!"

Mr. Stinson's eyes had never looked larger, or had a more welcoming shade of Blue. I looked back through his pop bottle lenses and felt honored to share a handshake with such a kindly old gentleman.

"Did you come in for a Bill Williams Hot link Lefty?" "I've never left here without one Cleatus!" We both laughed.

"Actually Mr. Stinson, what I come for was a piece of advice. I need someone to tend the chickens and look after my place for a week or so while I'm out of town. I need someone who won't burn the house down or let my chickens starve.

If you know anyone like that, he can have the run of the place while I'm gone.

Kory keeps the pantry stocked up and there's plenty of meat in the freezer."

"I've got just the one for you, Lefty, Ole Salberry Hagen. He's the kind what'll clean your truck and leave the change he finds in the floorboard, on your tailgate. True as a level and straight as a string, right as a rule he is… I've known him for the better part of 40 years.

Ole Salberry came in a few nights ago looking for a place to park his camper. I stretched him a cord and parked him out back. I won't have to put him up long. As long as I've knowed him, he's always been a rolling stone, a "fiddle foot," as you may say.

I'll chase him up if you want, he's right over there playing dominoes.

Cleatus pointed out to me an old cowboy who looked like he'd been rode hard and put up wet… not too different from myself.

I ate a Bill Williams Hot Link while Salberry Hagen rolled up his electrical cord and made ready for the trip to Jeter.

Kory made a sporadic turn into "Mother Clucker's Poultry Palace" without using her turn signal. I was afraid that after trying to keep up with Kory in the Jeep, he might turn around and just go on back to the Fish Camp.

As usually happens, me and Kory changed places in the drive thru so she could eat while I drove.

Just before the freeway "On Ramp," there was Ole Salberry waiting by the roadside with his emergency flasher's blinking a steady rhythm. I pulled up behind him and told Kory to offer him some chicken.

She looked at me reproachfully. "I only have two

pieces left!" "You don't have to give all of it to him Honey, just half with him what you have left.

Kory pouted momentarily, wondering if she was going to make a fuss over her chicken, or not? She wrapped the piece she was going to save for later in a napkin, and carried him the box.

We picked up Ole Blue the next morning from Poskey's Full Service with an oil change, a sparkling windshield and a full tank of gas.

Kory piled the passenger floorboard up level with Ole Blue's bench seat. Then she slid the cloth suitcase horizontally through the passenger door... it fit perfectly.

I sat Jazz atop the suitcase on the pillow Kory had provided for her comfort. Jazzy sat proudly as she looked out the windshield.

Jazz had a bird's eye view. She knew that on this trip, she would be the "Navigator." My best dog ever, put her front paws on the dash and perked her ears... she was on point!

Kory bitched the hump like a teenaged girl on her third date with a peach faced boy who had persuaded her only the night before to share her sweetness.

We were off to Rising Fawn, Georgia on a 693 mile trek with the potbellied stove from the railway station strapped securely up next to the cab of Ole Blue! We hit Interstate 70 East and kept on truckin' until evening came. Kory said she had good eyes for night driving and offered to take the wheel. I thought about it until Jazzy started spinning circles and biting at her pillow.

"Honey," I said. "We're in no big hurry. I must not have wiped very good this morning. I feel a bad case of, "red ass" coming on. After driving all day, I could sure use a good shower. Let's just get a motel room and head out fresh in the morning… Whatta' you think Babe?

A "Motel 6" Billboard and a "Waffle House" sign were my saving Grace. They came in sight just as we topped the next hill.

I was soon to find that Kory liked her hashed brown potatoes scattered covered and smothered, chunked, chopped and diced.

She reached down between her legs and snatched her purse. "I think I have a gift card for "Waffle House!"

Kory had a gift card for most everything. She flipped the lid on her recipe box and thumbed through her alphabetized "Gift Card" collection.

There must have been more than a hundred she'd collected from aspiring politicians in Kansas City.

Gleefully she plucked out the Waffle House gift card. "Here we go… Waffle House…25 dollars!

Her words were music to my ears. It meant that she wasn't going to drive, and I wasn't going to have to pay for dinner either!

TWENTY-SEVEN

Motel 6 was cheap and sleezy like the Jeter Inn. There's nothing like cheap and sleezy for a fuck-fest! Especially when you hear the couple next door pounding their headboard against your wall! There's nothing like the sound of another couple getting it on to put led in your pencil.

Hotels are prim and proper. It's easy to feel out classed by the arrogant assholes you run in to at the ice machine.

I figure cheap motels are like horseshoes. When a woman lets out a low moan howl, the man on the other side of the four-inch wall just made a "Ringer!"

The next morning, we ate a day-old doughnut and drank a cup of coffee. I guess Jazzy was the only one who got any sleep that night.

The ole boy in the room next door got more, "Hail

Merry's" than I did that night. I was feeling a little, "Out Done," as you may say.

Kory can tell you that I ran up the middle for a few touchdowns myself, but I didn't make M.V.P.

I felt much better about everything when I saw beer cans tied to their bumper... and "JUST MARRIED!" Painted on their window.

I'm not exactly sure how we ended up in Nashville. I guess that's what happens when you have a singing dog as your navigator? The street names were the same, but everything else had changed.

The Ryman Auditorium was still standing in good repair behind "Tootsies Orchid Lounge" on fifth Avenue North.

We drove down 16th Avenue on "Music Row." A street that is better known by those like myself as... "The Street of Broken Dreams."

We fought the traffic down Lower Broad until we came to the Cumberland River and took a right, back to Interstate 24. The sign read Chattanooga 133 miles.

When Kory saw the sign, she said: "That's where Gramps grew up, do you think we can still find Suck Creek?

Kory found my hand with hers. Her mouth had drawn down not in a frown but with the true look of want.

A woman is like a Diamond. I think that's why Diamond's are a girl's best friend. Like a Diamond, a woman has so many facets that don't show until you look at them in just the right light.

I lit a cowboy killer and took a hard pull. She was still looking at me with what I'd come to know as an unrelenting…"Pretty Please Baby."

I was as big of a fool as anyone on Kansas City's "Capitol Hill," when it came to Kory Katz.

"If the Tennessee River still runs through Suck Creek, we'll find it Baby! We'll ride Suck Creek Mountain all the way up to the Refuge. Who knows… maybe we'll even find a moonshine still?

Kory reached over and tickled my belly until we almost ran off the road. "Look Lefty, we're almost there!" She said pointing to the highway sign.

CHAPTER

TWENTY-EIGHT

We took a right hand turn off the interstate into Lookout Valley, then headed up the Lookout Mountain Parkway. The road was steep and wound halfway to the sky. Ole Blue was rolling steam from under the hood by the time we finally leveled off.

I wheeled into a gas station and popped the hood. Jazz tumbled out behind me and found a patch of grass. "Is Ole Blue okay?" Kory asked. "Yea, he just needs a cool drink of water and a minute to rest. You want a Mountain Dew?" I asked.

"No... but I need to pee." Kory pecked me on the cheek and headed for the restrooms while I squirted Ole Blue's radiator with a garden hose.

Kory brought me out a Mountain Dew even though I hadn't asked for one. Over the time we'd spent together, she had discovered that usually what I offered her, is what I wanted myself.

She put a leash on Jazzy, and they walked around while I tended Ole Blue. I was digging around in the back for a rag to put over the radiator cap when I heard a tumbling in the potbellied stove. "Hee! hee! Hey Wefty… are we dare yet?"

"Yes, we're in Rising Fawn, but not to the Cureton Plantation yet." "Oh man Wefty!

I'm almost home!"

The moon was only one day away from being full that night according to the farmer's Almanac. It was a silver moon that shone brightly in the thin cold mountain air.

The historical marker was just where Kory's yard sale Encyclopedia Britannica said it would be.

Kory's cat green eyes caught the silver moon as she read aloud from the historical marker. It told all about the Cureton Plantation.

"James and Nancy Cureton called their estate: "Dademont," she said as if her final curiosity had been satisfied.

"Keep Jazz here with you Honey. I'm gonna see if I can find anything left of the old waterwheel or the sawmill."

I walked down a dirt path that took me directly where I was going. In the moonlight I could see the remains of what was easily recognizable as a waterwheel. It stood stark and broken with the passage of time.

The heavy metal axle running through the wheel's center answered a question that had been on my mind since I loaded the stove on the truck with the motor hoist… how was I going to unload it? Now the answer was simple.

With everyone aboard, I backed Ole Blue under the axle and attached one end of the old yellow tow strap to it. I wrapped the other end around the stove, and drove out from underneath it!

"Hey Wefty! Easy Dude! There was Chucklehead popping in and out the stove door as it flapped while the stove swung wildly! Kory laughed so hard she had to hold herself to keep from peeing!

I settled the stove and released the ratchet on the strap. When the stove was settled on the waterwheel's concrete foundation, Chucklehead peeped out the stovepipe hole.

Kory and I sat on the tailgate in silence until Chuck finally spoke. "I'm home! I'm finally home!" His words rang true and clear without the slightest sign of his speech impediment. He rose from the stove like an angel robed in white.

Kory and I were transfixed as his Spirit glowed like a firefly. He gently waved goodbye and began to float up toward Heaven as if he were in no particular hurry.

Just when we lost sight of him, a falling star streaked across the sky. Kory leaned in close and said in a tearful whisper, "That star fell to make room for Chuck in Heaven. Chucklehead just found the light!"

THE END